SOFT TISSUE DAMAGE

Anna Whitwham

First published in 2025
by Rough Trade Books

First Edition

ISBN 978-1-914236-48-8

Design by Eliza Hart
at Office Of Craig

Printed in England

For my mum

Prologue

She is the blue corner. I don't look directly at the girl I am fighting. Not yet. I can tell her shape. Her wide, tank-body and stocky legs. She is skipping on the spot like she knows more than I do, the trick to holding your space in this ring. I lean back on the ropes as if I am calm, but my stomach pulses, driving a war from this belly.

I hear the judge announce the first round. We are to listen to the referee at all times.

Seconds out.

There is a moment, before we meet in the centre, this flash of recognition between us, the direct stare, as if we notice each other for the first time. A second where we could smile. If this was another time. Another place.

She wears make-up. Pretty, but she is ugly to me. I have to make her ugly. Her eyes lined too heavy. The smear and glint of petroleum.

I'm not wearing any. We have to hurt each other. I must hurt her. I imagine it already. A jab to splinter cartilage.

But the game plan is to keep her at distance. I am the taller boxer. I have the long arms. That's what makes sense.

Then the bell. The rush of blood and the crowd melting to murmur and it's just us. The ring is clean—it's ours—this quiet, crystal space.

I stalk her corner.

I jab and it's fierce enough to keep her stepping back. I throw a straight right—it is a power punch. She does the same and our gloves clash and scuff for a second, but my next jab lands clear and she teeters and walks backwards. I keep her away with the long jab of my left arm, herding her into the ring's corner. She lands against ropes, and I connect with a big right hand to her left cheek. It cracks the side of her head. She wobbles. It stops her. She falls back and looks to her corner for help. The referee counts her down from eight, and she finds her breath and a way to return. I should have hit her again. Another right to her head. Now we go back to corners for the second round. My punch to her head has buzzed her to rage and survival and she comes back wilder, wanting a tear-up, and I forget the things I'm good at. Instead of keeping distance, and throwing long, snappy jabs, I charge with her.

We have a tear-up. I keep replying to her punches. She has two shots, and she uses them over and over. A loopy overhand right to my head and a left to my body. She throws these over and over and I stop defending. I stop moving my head out of the way. I'm supposed to stick to my jab. All I have to do is drive her back—and keep that space. But we are smashing into each other. This is now just about toughness, not skill. Who can connect the hardest. Which of us can stay standing.

She cracks my right ear and immediately my legs collapse beneath me. I can hear the crowd make noise, a shock, and an excitement too. And then the buzz of white silence. I stagger into ropes. I try to comprehend it. I return to standing, my arms locked back into position. I can feel the fuzz, the echo of my skull as I follow her around the ring and throw shots. When the round is done, I can't hear what's being said to me in my corner. I nod to the woman talking as she drips water into my mouth. I'm slowing. The wires, snapped. My balance, it's shifted. My vision is slipping. I am only nodding to things I can't hear.

My daughter watches from the table. I can't see her. But there, in the dark, she witnesses this. I get up with whatever I have left. An urgent message from brain to body to stay moving. I must show her I am fine. I am fine. I feel nothing. I move beyond consciousness. I am not really here. The equilibrium has been punched out with her right hook. It has dislocated my step, my left leg feels longer than my right and I stalk, horse-like, punches in lunges. But they still land. Somehow, this is still a fight. I box from memory. I am able to make the referee think I'm still able to stay in the ring. I rock her again, but because I am fuzzy and slow, I can't move my own head out of the way and she lands another right to the side of my head, to the same ear. And it's too much.

I drop, broken.

I manage to stand again, I gaze up at the referee, at his gravel-nose and kind eyes. He looks at me like a father. He holds my shoulders. I know it's done. I say I can go again. I say something. In the moment it feels possible. I can keep going. He smiles—he is the thing that's keeping me up. He's whispering to me that it's over. I nod back to him, accepting this is it, as he counts down seconds to make it final and finished. It has to be over.

I wait for someone to take me out of the ring, I can't remember walking, or moving, or who is there to catch me.

I forget I have a daughter.

I forget how to walk. I am moved by other arms. I am slipping, falling into the person leading me back to the changing room. There is the bedlam of this ballroom, but I don't understand where I am. Only when I sit down and try to talk do I realise it's my daughter's father, bent down and staring into my face. Something stings on my skin and a medic sits in front of me and holds my wrist, shining a torch in my eyes. I feel desperate for my trainer. I see him walk in and maybe I imagine it but he's shaking his head. I have let him down. He says I did good. But I have let him down. I did everything wrong today.

I still can't talk, and a crowd of boxers hold me, an arm on each side, as if I can't be trusted to hold my own spine up. I search again for my trainer. I want him to tell me it's okay.

I drink a can of Coke because I'm told I need sugar and when I've filled my throat, I try to stand and find my feet. I manage it and wobble to the bathroom with my bag dragging the floor. There are grazes across my face, and my skin looks lashed and stung. My eyes, shattered. The ceiling light cuts at my eyeball. Small whip marks like split veins on my cheeks. I put jeans on, sitting on a toilet seat, pulling the denim over trembling legs. I take my hair out of the braids, and it sits stiff down my back, hard with hairspray. I draw red lipstick on my mouth, which has started to plump and swell.

When I go downstairs, I am aware of the way people stare at me. Surprised to see me walking. Sad to see my face this way. I stand in the middle of them, waiting for someone to come and talk to me. My head thrums. 'Where is my daughter? Where is Sylvie?' I ask anyone. Anyone should know. I need to see her. But they only keep staring, and I wonder what I'm doing for them to stare so much, until one of the older boxers comes over to take my bag and helps me to a sofa.

'Anna, you need to sit down. You're concussed.'

I

Mum's cancer came at the end of summer. We walked slow, through the canal's mineral light, away from the traffic and smoke of the hospital. Both of us quiet, waiting for the shock of prognosis to soften. We linked arms like little girls and then she went a few steps ahead to see two ducks fussing around their nest. She was going to die from this. This was fact. She turned to me, in shimmer and sun, smiling in her green linen dress. The creases still precise from the chair she'd sat on when they told us what was in her lung. The size of a tennis ball now. Why hadn't she come in sooner.

I was there the day she bought the dress. I said it was her colour. I told her to buy it.

It's in my blood to do it.

My grandad was a boxer in east London. He was a member of the Crown & Manor Boy's Club in Dalston until he died. Later he trained the army in fitness and fighting. It is still there, his old club, by the thick, black canal, and he—and that club—are the beginning of this. We look the same. I am the blue eyes, fair-freckled skin, and those bony, rangy shoulders. The long, slender fingers. I am his red hair. I am his boxer in the ring. His quick, fierce temper. We have a photograph of him on the bookshelf, his freckles smoothed out in sepia, a cowboy brow. His hands in the pockets of a wide-boy suit—or arms folded in starch-white vest, long, balletic when he let them hang by his side.

He was always getting into fights as a boy. His dad, Charlie—a labourer—led him down to the local boxing club because he'd run out of ideas and time. How could he keep him safe. The woodchips he was breathing in would give him stomach cancer before my grandad had turned 21, and maybe he knew he needed to put things in place—that some other father figure would be needed. It taught Grandad how to be precise with his temper. He took it to York Hall. He became an amateur boxer.

I lived with my mum when she was dying. I was there. It felt like she was always dying, after we got her diagnosis. Her life extended, but always in treatment. Always in cycles of hurt and healing. The chemotherapy trapping her in cycles of scans and smoggy walks to Charing Cross Hospital. The therapy almost killed her. Mum's kidneys stopped working and I spent twelve hours watching a monitor to see if she'd make it. She came out of her coma and died two years later. The final six months were brutal. I cleaned bed sores and helped carry her body, just bone and skin, out of the bath. I had to use my body to move hers. To clean hers—to feed hers. I used to lie beside her and pour teaspoons of morphine into her mouth, beak to baby bird.

I rubbed oil onto her cold, spiny shins because everything was cracking, splitting, weeping. I always tried to mend her on the surface. I couldn't get to the tumour, but I could seal wounds and wash hair. On the morning she died I continued rubbing cream into the arches of her feet. Always cycles of hurt and healing.

We cremated her in willow and rosehip and buried her next to Grandad. The grief was, it is, a total darkness. At its worst, it is ordinary. She isn't here, every day, and she will never be here again. It interfered with sleep—with all systems. I'd be woken by shakes, the shudder of this reality. I couldn't get past the cremation, imagining the heat stripping her down to bone, and then to ash. How she could cease to be, so quickly. I kept thinking we should have buried her whole. Then I could know there was an outline of her body somewhere beneath the soil. I could seek out the shape of her. Eventually I began to lose hair.

My trainer finds me at this point.

I stumble into his gym's boxing night when watching my daughter's musical theatre class. The boxing and dance school share a venue. The men are exciting, but it is the women. I have never seen so many women boxers before. Braided, muscled, my age and younger, walking into the changing rooms. Some nod at me, some look at the floor. They look self-possessed, together. They don't smile. I want to know them. I want to ask how they got so tough—how they got their grace and power. How they got to feel so at home in their bodies.

'You want to fight?' He asked it slightly joking. Shorter than me, Marine-toned and sharp, he said it so easy it almost made sense. He said it like it was already going to happen.

2

Only in evenings did she falter, tears in her eyes for a second, as it must have all come horribly clear to her. She turned to me and said she wasn't ready to not have me around. She wasn't ready for me to leave her. It was my life she wouldn't get to know in her death. She wouldn't know my sister's babies. She wanted my sister to have babies. That's what made her so sad.

The gym is like a secret. Small, busy and hidden under arches. The music is loud, and the boxers mind their own business on the bags. The smell of the bleach that strips equipment of its sweat, gets stuck in clean knots at the back of my throat.

When I go there for the first time I think of my grandad, the way boxing found him when he had diphtheria. The way he held himself in tweed, Hamlet cigars between his teeth. I used him for courage. I copied his toughness.

The trainer I met at the fight night isn't here today. Instead, I have one of the other coaches. He wears a purple beanie and is reading a book on the bike machine when I arrive. He knows it's my first time. He suggests they're all learning in this boxing gym. I can hear the whip-quick thrash of fists on a bag and feel brand new to this.

There is a sense of ceremony when moving into the ring for the first time, perhaps every time, the dipping of the body, and standing tall again, the emerging into new space. The light makes spots on the black vinyl floor. I can see myself in the mirror. I wait for him to tell me to start hitting, I'm keen to start hitting. But we don't. In fact, the gloves I'm borrowing stay outside of the ring. I have to remember this is a trial. It's not the real thing.

My trainer asks me to show him how I jab, and he looks at the angles, the lines, the way my body turns. His arms are folded, and he steps back. I am corrected instantly, on the way I stand, the way I move when I punch from my elbow—awkward and weak. I laugh when I'm corrected because it is so unusual, to be touched and realigned with such care. My body doesn't want to be bent this way and rejects the corrections. Springing back to stiffness.

'You ever shadow-boxed?'

I'm fixed to where I stand—I am only silhouette. I don't know what shadowboxing is.

This trainer folds his arms and waits. He is calm—serious.

'It's just you and your shadow. These are the basics.'

I try to fill the silence, the space, talking to eat up the clock.

'I did ballet. I used to dance.'

As if this is my excuse to stand still.

But this doesn't help me now, I'm unable to move my feet and my body looks silly. One of the other trainers sits and looks to see what I might do next. When I do nothing, he turns back to his bag, his face is bruised, glinting fish scales. He wears them as if they are just skin. His ribs like wheels when he hits the bag, his back slicing air when his shoulders roll. The hiss and groan from somewhere in his gut. When he moves, he sings with it, as if he is the only person here.

'It doesn't have to look perfect.'

There are three minutes on the clock, three minutes blinking backwards in red lights.

'Go on.' And then, kindly, 'just try.'

The neon numbers are blinking quickly, and the urgency of this presses at something. I am still shuffling, awkward, and now I am aware I am wasting time. As a gesture I try jogging on the spot a little, throwing jabs gently, pointlessly. I won't be able to fill a minute up. I can't move into its space. I won't be enough.

He tells me to try and line the punches up with my own head. To use the mirror as more than reflection. To see myself as an opponent, moving in time with me—my shadow. I have to try and cut into this silhouette.

'You have to move with her. You have to find her.'

He resets the clock.

'Go again.'

I am starting to sweat, and I make new shapes. I want to distort the woman in the mirror. She shudders and steps closer. She looks so fucking stupid. I fumble something in the air, making fists and shapes, until eventually these violet beams become moonlight and I am lost in the poetry of this. I can hear my breath when I move, the *hiss-bap* sound from my mouth. As if I am the only person here.

'It gets easier. You'll get the fundamentals.'

Still calm, still serious.

When I collect my daughter from school, she runs out to get her hug. I am pleased to see her so happy and so messy—her hair is out of its band and her hands are tattooed with ink from an art lesson. I buy her a pink, iced doughnut. She leaves me the last bite and shows me a scrape on her hand from a fall at break time. It is barely there, but it stings. She tells me the plaster fell off. I look at her little bruises and scrapes, her knees always healing from some playground game. She demands plasters for all her wounds. She likes to layer them on—three at a time. She is loud about it, when she is hurt, she cries. It is the shock, not the pain. That's why she cries. I wipe the jam sugar from her mouth and kiss her warm head.

'There are more plasters at home.'

That is enough for her. The promise that I will cover the places she hurts.

When we get home, she takes off her uniform, grabbing clothes from her dressing-up basket and leaving a trail of slips, fake-fur and my old high heels along the corridor. She settles on a flamenco skirt and a pair of gold heels I found in a vintage shop. Her toes grip the shoes as she walks, and the heels scrape the wooden floor. She knows she is only allowed five minutes in heels. That's my rule. To save her ankles and back. She lounges on pillows, feet propped up. Only the single scar on her knee from a toddler fall marks her body. She observes her toes, lifting her leg up and down. She seems to know her body so well already.

I see my reflection in the window, as evening falls to dark, spotted in ceiling light. I am cooking, but I pause. I throw a jab; I bow my head. Even alone, I am still self-conscious.

I order my first pair of boxing gloves. They are black, and cheap enough to throw away if I get bored.

I go back two days later. My original trainer is now back, and we have a session together. He was in the Marines and reminds me of my grandad: polite, kind, but tough. We connect, immediately. He is the right fit. He has trained everyone. There is no small talk or fake praise. We focus on muscle memory. I have to throw jabs in the mirror, on a bag, and then pads. Over and over, again and again. Until it's locked. Built into the tissue. I am sure he has seen the glinting scars on my arm under the pallor of these white lights, but he says nothing. They are twenty years old and have never faded. I did them to myself.

I don't tell him my knuckles are starting to sting because my wraps are too thin. Each time I hit with my right I shudder a little, but I don't want him to know it hurts. He can't know I'm struggling this soon. It is only my second time. He will make me rest, or come back tomorrow, and I don't want to do that. I don't want him to make me stop—for me to not finish this round—so I punch harder because I think maybe my knuckles just need to be roughened more, made into better fists. I try to train my body to feel pain. I feel pain in silence.

I have just seen the English National Ballet with my oldest friend. The bodies move satin in air, the feet staccato, the muscles ripping silently, beautifully. The toes, bent, bloodied knots. My friend was a ballerina, and I know her feet have been mauled. My daughter will go on points soon if she continues to dance. For a while she will dance on blood as her toes harden.

'Did you see the way it's in two parts? The body levitates above the snap of the feet. They move together, like bird wing.'

She speaks this language and I ask her if she thinks there is something linked between ballet and boxing.

'Oh definitely. There is the pleasure-pain. To make your body do something so beyond what it should. And to make it beautiful.'

She says a boxer is their body. Like a dancer is their body.

When the pain keeps beating in my right hand, I try and read it as growth. I can feel scraped, wet skin. The boys on the bags are punching hard and I don't want to be the girl who gives up. They are completing rounds of press-ups and planks. Steam rising from their backs, dented, and scalloped with muscle and effort. One has cigarette burns on his back.

'You have a lot of power. You could hurt someone. Knock them out.'

There is another trainer lost in the bliss and ritual of punching the bag. Each crack on leather takes him out of his head and into his body. Healing, tea-marks of a bruise case his left eye. I smile and stop punching as hard. I move to the floor to try out a journeyman hook—a punch that comes round, wide, in a loop, to catch my opponent in the head.

I find a corner, where they stack the weights, just by the toilet. Away from the boys and their backs. I have halved myself in the thinnest slice of mirror. I have made myself small, a little invisible. I move without commitment, holding my breath. I want this to be over, to go home.

'What are you doing?'

My trainer has seen me.

'Why are you standing over there, in the corner?'

It is a genuine confusion. I motion to the three boys who are now stretching and smiling, easy with their square foot of floor to ease their muscles.

'I didn't want to be in their way.'

He steps onto the floor. He has been drinking his mug of coffee, changing the music. There are always songs here. Elvis, or Bad Bunny—whatever the boxers want.
'Don't move out the way for them.'

'I'm sorry.'

'If you say sorry again, I'll make you do 50 press-ups.'

The scars are not the thing to be ashamed of. It's the disappearance. It's the hiding them. This is not the place to make myself smaller.

That night my daughter wakes and walks down the hall. She climbs beside me. Her hand finds mine, and I look at her perfect nose, the stenciled eyes. The painted mouth. She is in blossom, alive. There is a little vein on her neck, beating like wing against sleep. I think of all the things that could hurt her. The ways her face could bruise. I never want her to die. I remember a friend telling me she imagined her child falling off a cliff, constantly, and how this was nature's way of making sure she kept her safe. And my own mum, taking that phone call, when I was crying to her from the Half Moon pub, my nose almost broken and stuffed with blood.

'Dad will have to come and get you.' So angry with me, but so angry with him, the man she couldn't hurt back on my behalf. So angry it had happened. She could only whisper. 'I'll see you at home.'

I go back to the gym the following week, and the week after that. Each time I get better. After a month I buy myself better gloves, better wraps too. I start to punch from the shoulder, and the punches feel powerful.

Once a week I am here, my hair spun in a clip. I wear mascara and perfume and chains around my neck. I'm not ready to let go of those ornaments yet. I still want to feel pretty.

A young boxer pauses to ask how I am finding it all. I tell him more than I do my close friends. He asks if it's harder for me to fight because I haven't given myself permission yet. He has just lost a fight and he is more solemn, quiet. I say I'm not sure.

I say sorry when I leave. My trainer tells me to stop saying it. Correct your mistake and carry on. Hold your space. My mascara has smudged, and I wipe the smeared grease into my sweat. He makes another joke about me fighting. I laugh.

'Anyone can fight, Anna.'

But I don't think they can. I don't think I can.

3

We often met in the kitchen for tea when day broke into blue. The pain had started to wake her up and I'd hear her slippers on the stairs and they'd wake me up too. She would lean on the counter, her back to me, waiting for the click of the kettle. We could hear owls outside. The dawn cold and new. Always a biscuit at the table, dunked in weak and milky tea where she'd taken the bag out too soon. We never finished the tea. It wasn't about the tea; it was about the time. We knew sleep would come and we had nowhere better to be than here. When she was in her bed, I would check on her, make sure she had breath. Then back to my room, wondering if I should check another time, to hold that image over, of her drifting, mouth parted, her chest only slightly rising with heartbeat.

I stop training for the summer because my daughter has been accepted to dance with Dance Theatre of Harlem and we spend July in New York.

We are headed home on the A train, getting back to Brooklyn, sipping on iced fruit teas from Dunkin' Donuts that are too big to finish, both of us struggling with bucket-size cups and the swampy July heat. I see the famous Gleason's boxing gym is on the corner—close to where my sister lives and where we are staying. I have to visit. It feels like going to church. I am not dressed the right way. New York in July is tropical, and my body feels swollen, my blue velvet ballet shoes reddening my heels. My dress sticks to every dip and curve of my body, slapped to the sweat of my back. It's a painful heat. I take my daughter's hand and parade a little, walk into the gym's corners, having a long look at the walls of photographs and posters, which are a walk of fame. They are all here. I spot Tyson. The gold tooth smile. The wall is signed by Muhammad Ali—a small scribble you'd never notice. I touch the place his hand touched. This gym has looked after everybody.

I meet Bruce. The man who runs Gleason's—and has run it since the 1980s. I tell him I box. I sit beneath the fan in his office, my daughter at my side, scribbling in her notepad. She is endlessly patient with me in public.

'It doesn't matter how good women are, or how good they get. They'll never want them out of the kitchen.'

He is a small, brilliant man, in a red wool hat, even in this heat, drinking from a can of Coke. When I ask about the women who train here, he says they make up the largest number of clients, and the fighters are from everywhere—they have PhDs and modelling contracts—the point he's making is that anyone and everyone comes here.

Women were banned from fighting professionally until 1996 because they had periods. It feels an ancient rule, but it isn't at all. It was a rule made up in my lifetime.

Bruce asks if I want to fight here, and I do. He books me into a session the following day.

When I come back, I am dressed in leggings and a vest. On my way in I see the fighter, Heather Hardy, training for a fight. She's 40, like me, with a daughter—a single mother too. Pin-up pretty and blonde. I go up to her when she's taking a break and she sees my ponytail and the shades in my hand, and I know she must think I am there to stage photos—to play pat-a-cake with the pads. All I can do is tell her she inspires me.

'Enjoy your stay,' in her twisting Brooklyn whisper.

For the first time I spar, with my trainer, an old pro in a wool hat. We wear headguards and it feels fun. I like how we play together. My punches thrash and crawl but there are combinations. I am in some control. Until I'm not and he announces it's 'his turn' and I get belted across the head. It hurts. Sylvie sits at the corner of the ring rolling the little weights and sipping water.

There is an audience now. A fighter I recognise stands with his arms folded. He looks unimpressed. I am told about the fighter's life as we settle back into the ring for another round.

He was supposed to become a professional but got caught in a
street fight after playing pool and lost sight in one eye. A career
stopped short, now he trains and runs his own gym. He is hard to
please.

'Show up,' he yells at me. 'Show UP.'

I punch harder knowing I'm being watched. I think of everything
I have, and I give it all. I do good—enough to earn handshakes.

'You're strong, but your feet are no good.'

I see the fighter at the end when I'm cooling down. I make the
mistake of telling him it's frightening to spar—how scared I was
to do it.

'If you're frightened get a dog.'

I wish I'd kept quiet. I feel stupid. I take another walk to cool
off. I can't stop sweating.

I spot him. He's there, above some red piping: Jack Dempsey.
The low brow, the ink-eyes—the black vest and shorts. The
boxer's boxer. He was greatness. My grandad borrowed so much
of it; wanted to be this hero. Both he and Mum kept telling me
always to be frightened but do it anyway. Walk into the room.
Make the noise.

I circle back and am happy to see my daughter chatting happily and with ease to the fighter, like she's fixing the mess I made. She's telling him she's half-Irish. She tells him she is a dancer too.

'I know some good Irish fighters. John Duddy—those guys. You guys are good at fighting.' He talks to her like a real person. Like she really exists to him.

She smiles and nods. Her face has caught sun. She is honey— and there are freckles.

'I'm Sylvie Poppy O'Brien.'

Already entitled to it—the compliment, her inheritance—herself. She thinks, maybe, that she's one of them.

The trip is the turning point. I did it. I am less afraid. My body is changing, enough for me to notice. No one else would know. But I see the shoulders bigger; I am losing softness. I love my new shape. The old, dead fat of me is being chiselled at—broken down. The way it sweats and the way I walk slower, taller.

I find the time to go to the gym twice a week, in between work and being a mother, it becomes the thing I look forward to the most. I make my week work around boxing. One day I am asked if I want to fight. My trainer says it so casually, almost a throwaway offer, and I have to catch it—do I want to fight on the next show. He tells me to take the weekend to make my mind up because our training will change a lot. We will start camp. It won't be for play anymore. I go to sleep on Friday night imagining myself throwing jabs, my body dreaming itself there. I shadow box in my sleep, holding fists of light.

4

It moved, travelled. It began to press against her throat so that she couldn't swallow. This was why she hadn't been able to eat. Why she had lost all the weight. We knew she wouldn't be leaving this hospital. When she was in her bed I'd watch her clutch at her chest, fingers pressing at a hollow place where the hurt came from. The wait for morphine, those minutes as the nurse came and spoon-fed her the relief, and then watching her holding on until it swam into the veins and softened her face. Mum called the night nurse 'Irish John'. He was scruffy, tired, and always remembered Mum's name. He was her nightcap, her bedtime story. I'd watch them through the thick glass, at how grateful she was when he took her wrist, blueish and bruised from needles, twisted the feed and added the fluids and morphine. 'It was unacceptable for her to be in pain,' he said. 'Irish John' was more important than any of us. She held his arm and he waited until her head was comfortably sunk into her pillow, tucking her in, moving aside her clumsy feed and wheels, with all its muck and clutter.

I am back in London, and I tell my trainer I'll do the fight. New York has made me think I can do it.

The tone changes. His face a frown. It's not a game anymore. He is back in the Marines, leading men. He tells me about camp and what this means for me. It all feels official.

He takes me for a walk to buy me a tea and we sit in comfortable silence.

'Will I get hurt?'

He has ordered us each a stir-fry.

'You need to eat.'

I am not hungry. I can't eat. I am imagining what it will feel like, to walk in front of 300 people and to stand under white lights and to hit someone else. A final way to stand up for myself.

'But will I be hurt?'

I don't know what I expect him to say. To lie—to say getting hit doesn't hurt.

'Maybe,' he says.

'There's always a risk. You'll definitely get hit.'

We don't talk about pain.

We walk back to the gym, and he tells me I look pale. I think I am in shock. I try warming my hands up. I can't get warm. When we are back the mirrors have steamed and some of the other trainers are running sessions. I tell one of them, the one I can talk to—bruising water-marked on his face.

'You'll love it,' he tells me and I wonder if it's true. 'You'll get hit. But you'll hit her more.'

I pick at my nails. My hands are still in wraps.

'Get in the ring. Gloves on.'

I think this is it. I am going to start fighting today.

But instead, he tells me I am going to learn how to absorb pain. To let my body learn how to live with it.

'Otherwise, you'll just be frightened of getting hit.' He takes a pause, changes the music. 'And you are going to get hit.'

We work on the ways I can handle pain. I need to lean into my trainer's body—get close—it's an intimacy that means you have to feel comfortable in your body and skin. You need to let someone else take all your weight, your smell—your sweat and noises. I'm closing into the punch—the idea is that my shoulder takes the hit, not my face, or jaw. My first reaction is to move out of the way. Leaning into pain is a discipline.

It stings at first, but then it doesn't. Then the hurt is hardly there.

'I'm getting you used to being hit. Because you are going to get hit.'

He keeps saying it.

'You're going to get hit.'

There are two times I have had bruising on my face. The first time I was punched outside the Half Moon pub in South London at 15. The busted nose received admiration from other girls at school. I couldn't cover the swelling. Girls flocked around the old blood like birds, asking how much it hurt. Telling me how tough I was to have fought a man.

The second was when a heavy door was kicked so hard at my head my eyes shrank into their swelling and I could hardly see. It was an accident. I covered the bruises up with layers of make-up in case anyone thought I'd been beaten up. The bruised skin blotted back to the surface every so often and I would reapply the foundation thickly, only for it to return again. I learned that bruises are actually very hard to cover up. There is always some shadow. My male colleagues looked at me a little longer, looking for what was really there, behind the make-up. I saw photos of myself at Winter Wonderland—a work night out for Christmas—my skin still in its white shock.

The browning between my eye sockets so dark. I lived apart from Mum then, and she never saw my face. I made sure she didn't see. I avoided her for two weeks until I'd mended.

When she died, I had to contact her ex-partners to let them know and I felt shy and privileged when they told me how much they had loved her and sent me photographs of Mum before she was a mother, bronze in sepia photos with dark, smoked eyes. I had to comfort them, because I was the closest thing they had to her, and they'd never got to say goodbye. There are love letters. There are histories. Mum had lived in France. She'd been the first to go to university in her family and found her way to Marseille. We all admired the long, model legs she wrapped in black Joseph jeans. She bought three pairs because she said, 'that's what you did in France—you buy three pairs of the thing you love to wear the most.' There were other things she said... that her miscarriage was 'probably a good thing' because she was with a man who 'pulled her hair'. She said this so flippantly—just a passing comment, except I never forgot the image of Mum holding the wrists of a man who had her hair in the grip of a fist. I have a photograph of her in a fur coat, her face in a bright smile. She had looked so beautiful to me. But she told me to put the picture away. 'I wasn't happy then. I don't want to see myself then.'

Weeks after one of my miscarriages in my 20s we walked arm in arm along the Thames, following the looming water into lights. I had stayed with her for a week—she fed me blocks of dark chocolate and hot tea. She had watched me walk into the hospital room, I turned to see the blur of her face through the glass window watching me walk to the place where they took the rest of the pregnancy away. She said thinking of me alone was unbearable. She would have taken my place.

Her toughness was known. A family trait. When she'd been pregnant, a man had broken into the house, and she'd chased him down the road, barefoot. I think of the fight-flight as an expectant mother and how her body was becoming my body; the same way hers became her mother's body. Years later she had a fight with a mugger. She must have been in her 50s, because I was in my late teens. She pulled him to the floor until he got up and ran away. We all told her off.

'I wasn't letting go. He wasn't going to frighten me,' she said, breathless, her navy dress hitched up on one side when she came back to the house. Her shaking hand was still fixed to the broken strap of her handbag. My dad started making her tea, telling her she had too much of her father's streak and temper and had to be more careful.

When I called my parents as that 15-year-old girl from the south London pub where a man had just hit me, it was surprising that she handed the phone to my dad. That it was him who came to get me in a taxi. I expected her to drive down. Instead, she had waited for me at home—quiet in her rage that I'd put myself in a place of such danger. For her, this had come after a series of other events she hadn't been able to save me from: seizures in clubs—

truanting from school. All my self-harm too. This was another messy thing.

But when I woke, she came to my bed with coffee and toast and held my hand, her eyes searching my face for any permanent damage.

'I wish you could find some calm. I wish you were happier.' So close to me, she wanted to take my place.

She winced at the scars on my arm in summer, annoyed they wouldn't disappear. 'They're fading,' she promised me, and herself. When we both knew the sun seemed to only make them more pronounced and thicker.

I instinctively pull away and hold my left hand up to protect myself when my trainer takes aim at my shoulder. The danger here is that I'll ricochet back to my own cheek and cause more damage. That I will punch myself and hurt a cheekbone. I am learning how to box, which is different to fighting. I am not as scared of being hit as I thought. Today, when I slip into the punches I sit deep into my hip and turn so I can make space and counter with my left hook. It's on the count of three each time and the repetition of these shots make me sweat. It stings, but it doesn't sting that much.

'I'll see you tomorrow.' I pack my stuff. I feel my shoulder hot and hold my bag on the other side. 'Go and rest.'

My daughter is struggling at school. There is a problem girl in the playground. She shouts and barks at Sylvie. My daughter says she is fine and doesn't want to play 'unicorns' but this unkindness begins to press on her, I can tell. She has tantrums at home. Today my daughter has been pinned against the wall by the problem girl who holds her by the collar and demands she is given the snacks I pack for her. I tell my daughter to go gently, to ignore—to understand this girl doesn't have the same way of thinking—is unable to calm herself. My daughter's father is different to me. His background resolves disputes in a much quicker and maybe in a much cleaner way. As a teenage boy he had quick, wild fights with other local boys and shook hands after. He tells her she has the option of hitting back if she wants to. She doesn't have to—he doesn't say she should, but he says she can. She has the option if she needs it.

At first, I object. I don't want her to become that child. Violence doesn't solve anything. I am sure it doesn't. Except I start to wonder how far her empathy and silence will protect her and maybe the idea of violence being an option is helpful. I don't know why I am ruling it out. She can choose it if she wants to. If I had known I could fight back, then I would have. When I was punched in my face, I met the man's stare first. He knew what he was doing—and where he was aiming. I wasn't his accident. We met in that split second before—awake, alert—he wasn't so out of his mind. I have laughed and glossed over it all these years later, mocking the man for having a weak shot—for hitting a girl like 'a girl'. But it did hurt. And it was hard enough to bring swelling and blood, and even if it hadn't, I was punched. There are many times I wonder what would have happened if I'd hit him back.

When I get home, I pack my daughter into my bed with warm milk and a hug and a film. She is still distracted by the playground, I can tell. The girl screamed in her face today, and it's upset her. She doesn't know where to put this rage. When I'm in the bath I soak my body in salts and look at my shoulder. It's already coming up in purple knots—a shade for each of the ways I absorbed the hits. I feel vibrant and alive and powerful. I feel I'm working for something.

My daughter comes in, as she often does when I'm in the bath. She tells me about her day and makes up dances. I am her captive audience, sat in salts and water. She likes to look at my body, to see an image of herself, and she glances at my stomach, my hair, my moles. The scars on my arm I lie about.

I did this with my mum too. Sitting at her feet, or at the edge of sinks, talking, listening. The day I wept when she said she'd have her freckles until she died. Because until then I thought she'd live forever.

Sylvie notices my bruises straightaway and touches my shoulder with her little fingers, tracing the different patterns to soothe, which hurts a little, but I don't let her know. She asks what happened. These markings don't belong here. She knows I box; she has just seen me spar in New York. But she has never seen me bruise. She is concerned. She knows what a bruise feels like.

I tell her I was defending myself—protecting my body. I say it doesn't even hurt. Because it's true, it doesn't. Then I tell her it hurts a little bit—like a pinch. Because I don't want her to take her own pain too lightly. This bruising isn't a secret, and it isn't shame. I chose it, I reassure her. Because I am a good fighter and can understand that this bruise means I stopped bigger, harder punches. I don't know what I'm teaching her—that there are different ways to be hit, some better than others. I worry. I try to make better sense and bring it back to boxing.

'It means I won't ever break. I won't get knocked down.'
She keeps her hand on my shoulder, her fingers stroking the little blue and black spots, where blood has broken. And I feel bad, for making her worry. I quickly correct myself.

'Bruises don't make you strong. You don't have to get hurt like this to be tough.'

I turn the hot tap off because she wants to join me, and I make room for her little body to sit between my legs. She has done this since she was born. She leans on my knee. She is all muscle and dance, her limbs and her bones thin. One day she will be too old and too tall for this. She will disappear from me and guard her body from the world. But for now, she wants to sit in this water. She will be taller than me. Stronger than me.

5

They kept trying to find ways to place a feeding tube into Mum's body so that she could eat food. It would mean a longer life—an extended life. A sweet doctor promised Christmas, which was three months away. We were excited. Three months felt like forever. At first, they considered operating and sewing it in her stomach, but there was too little of her, and the tumour was pushing upwards, against gravity. They settled on a tube from her nose. Mum had been distressed, upset. She had always been beautiful. She asked me if she looked hideous, with the plastic tube moving food from the bag to her nose, and to her stomach. Her perfect nose still the same. Only her face, smaller, hair scraped back in the ponytail I'd washed, brushed, and tied. Being clean was all she wanted. To be clean and comfortable. Even then, she still believed she was going to go back out in public. That her legs would find their walk, and she would return to life. She could still drink tea—she still wanted to drink tea—and I went to the hospital kitchen to make us both fresh cups in saucers. The nurses let me do it.

We all had to get used to the feeding tube. The gurning, rolling sounds of the machine pumping the food into Mum, little by little, through her nose. Startling her, oozing a meal into her system. She had to pick the feed up with her fingers to drink the tea and it was such a struggle. For the first time I didn't know if staying alive was best for her.

I trust my trainer with my body. He sees so much of me up close: my skin, my scars, my faults. Through each menstrual cycle, when I turn up, heavy, exhausted, swollen with fatigue, and make mistakes. Now I am training I need to know he is there, always. Now I need him more than anyone—I need him to not let me falter, pause, consider my own fear too deeply. I need him to say everything is okay.

Today we organise our camp schedule. This is where I'll need to train harder, better, for eight weeks. I'll be training three times a week—a one-to-one, an hour of fitness—and sparring—which I've never done in London. He explains sparring will be like mock-fighting. It's tapping, more than hitting. Trying to find target spots. In New York I was in a headguard. Here there is a mouthguard only. I thought it was to stop teeth getting broken, but I'm told it stops a fighter biting into their own tongue.

My mouthguard isn't custom-made, so my trainer has taken me for coffee at the local café. He asks for a cup of boiling water and a glass of cold water. He times it all, his phone a stopwatch—he says this is what he did in the Marines. He arranges it all on the table and gives me instructions. The mouthguard goes into the hot water and then straight into my mouth. I bite down, meshing it to the grooves of each tooth. The water burns into the nerves, and I feel it shooting through my jaw, but I suck and bite and wait for his signal to stop. Then he takes it from me, straight from my own mouth, I am his baby, he is holding my spit. He is my mother.

He drops it in the cold glass of water. When the minute is up, he presents it to me. It's a perfect fit. Made for my mouth.

We have performed a ritual. It takes such care, such time, I know why boxers stay with their coach until the end. It is profound, transcendental. The trust, the care, is so precise, so constant. The more we train the more I trust him. I trust the timing of his decisions, the advice he gives—the way he wraps my hands and tells me to have days off. I respect and appreciate the way he nudges into my personal life only in the breathless, minute breaks between rounds, to check I am okay—to see where my head is at. Never to probe, or push—he is interested, but not intrusive. And it's the same the other way. I ask about Afghanistan, but at a distance. We have a coffee—an americano and cortado—and we return to the gym. One of the strong female fighters is training. I smile and watch her on the pads—she always hits with thunder.

I practice on the speedball, a ball on a pivot that flips quickly when tapped. It's tricky, to hit lightly and in a rhythm that meets the ball as it swings back. My trainer makes me do it with my eyes closed—it's my thinking that makes the mistakes. My body knows what to do. It works, every time.

We move to the harder punching bags, to nail my double-jab, over and over. It hurts, to get it good. We drill it and drill it, and then when my shoulder is burning with repetition, we stop. He says it's time to get into the ring.

The woman is already in there. She is a little bigger, her body built more squarely and compact and she wears a bandana to keep her hair back. I am in a huge T-shirt given to me by an old fling. He was an athlete, and it swallows me. I look bigger than I really am. I didn't know I was going to spar today. I knew it was coming, but not when. The surprise is deliberate. I don't have time to worry. I scoop my hair into a ponytail and fit my new mouthguard.

I'm told this is to get me out of my comfort zone. My chest is tightening. I've seen this woman fight in tournaments and she always wins. She's good—she comes in at her opponent, and she's clever. Once her opponent knelt down in defeat. A sign of boxing weakness. I don't know why she wants to box, to do this, or why she's here. But I know in this gym there are levels, and she is one of the best.

Her body is the opposite of mine. I'm rangier, my arms longer. This is my grandad's body, his arms, his shoulders.

I have been doing my Ancestry family tree after Mum's death. It keeps her alive and I worry we will be forgotten if I don't—my mum, her family, my London history. For 300 years I trace them back to Islington and Hackney. Poppy after Poppy—they stayed tight in their map. I find out my great-grandad, my grandad's father, was in a Holborn workhouse as a child, at nine. The same age as my daughter. I think about what echoes and ripples into bloodlines—watering down but still travelling. That pale rage. My grandad's fight to split from a culture of being poor—my mum carrying this with her without knowing it was even there. My grandad's tweed and waistcoats were a toughness, but they were a kind of servitude too. He was always wanting to fit into the other classes, which is why we never knew about Charles Poppy and the workhouse. Maybe he was never told, because by then it was just history. In the print of a family tree, it seems so close in time—so overlapped—as if I could pluck a name like they were contacts in a phonebook. Still reachable, still able to speak. But there are lifetimes between the Holborn workhouse and Grandad's pear trees in his Hertfordshire garden. When I went to study at UCLA on a scholarship, I would speak to Grandad on the phone once a week as I walked through Hollywood pine, kicking white-gold dust and I knew he was so proud of me. That I went on such an adventure. How far he had gone to have a granddaughter in California. He would ask for postcards just to see that stamp. I wonder if he would see my boxing as a step backwards. He wouldn't have wanted me to repeat the things he left behind.

I think my trainer looks nervous for me. He keeps telling me I'm going to get hit, as if by saying it over and over means I will become numb to this as fact. He wraps my hands and tells me to breathe. I am happy that he still does this. I could do my own, but he's always done it. It's a closeness I wish to keep. A loyalty, a friendship. He binds me together.

It is my first realisation of how lonely boxing is. My trainer can look after my body in the corner. He can be at my side, my closest friend here, when I'm standing outside the bell, but when I walk to the centre, touching gloves, staring into her face, I'm on my own. Boxing shows you exactly who you are. He tells me to get my range, to throw my jabs, and I'm nodding but then the two minutes start and I'm walking away from him, and I'm on my own. And it's happening. I'm doing this.

I am tentative at first, I want to see how she throws, but I need to see how my body behaves. If my legs move or stay fixed to their space. They don't. I move lightly, comfortably. I'm surprised by the way I move, keeping distance, making space. I move and then I jab, but it doesn't connect. Not yet. She holds her arms in front of her body and is compact, rocking herself side to side, keeping her head off the line. But the act of throwing gives me confidence and I go again, double, and it lands. We are only allowed to jab in this round, and it works to my advantage—my height helps. I jab and move, learning about my power—my left arm—seeing it come to life away from pads. When the two minutes is up, I haven't been hit. I have two rounds to go. A couple of other trainers jump up to the ring and watch. I stand still in this single minute. I catch breath. I turn down water. I'm told to move my head more.

We go again and this time we can throw more than jabs—double jabs to head and body. I start to feel my rhythm. I almost enjoy it, the game of chess, of pause and feint and sending a jab like a whip to her head. I know I am holding back. I am still scared to hit her, or anyone, in their face. And I find out this is dangerous—for me, not my opponent. Because I am tentative, unsure, about my own attack, I don't consider my own defence. I don't move my head, I don't step off the line, and halfway through the round I get hit in the middle of my face. My eyes water. I step back. It stuns me.

'You're bleeding.'

I can hear my trainer. I wipe my shoulder and leave a red trail on my T-shirt.

What surprises me, in the moment, is that it hurts, but it doesn't hurt enough. I don't want to stop.

'You alright?'

I nod, and step back to centre, moving a little quicker with my jabs, wanting to reassert my body in this space. I can feel it swelling, where she hit me. A fluffy pain. A deep cold that sits in my head. I tell myself if I don't hit back, I won't do this again. I have to tell my body it's still safe. I land a good jab to her body, and she feels it. It's enough for now.

My trainer checks I'm okay. Last round, open spar. We can throw anything. The knock to my face must have done something because I move into this last round a little more cautious. Now I have to protect from her right hand too. I use mine, but it's weaker than my left. I throw a one-two and get a clap from one of the trainers. But really, this round is one to get through, rather than show skill. I am nervous, and I do everything I can not to get on the receiving end of her right hand, which I have seen in practice and in fights. One nosebleed feels enough today.

When two minutes is up, I lean on the ropes with relief, my heart banging, muscles mixed with fatigue and adrenalin. I stayed out of the way.

I take my gloves off; they feel heavy and clumsy now. I wipe my nose and the blood spreads onto the pink hand wrap. I show it off.

'Look,' I tell three trainers. There are often trainers lined up to watch a spar. Their heads over the rope, nodding, making mental notes. They usually have a fight coming up. My voice slurps through the mouthguard. They nod, pleased in a way only we can all understand.

'You're a warrior.'

They've all had much worse. I've seen them walk in with deep cuts to their brow. A minor nosebleed is usual. It's a little experience. Impact is education. Impact over time makes features more swollen, more broken—you can tell a boxer's face, the bent, spud-nose. There is no pretending the hurt doesn't and cannot happen.

Before women boxed, when it was only men in the ring, Hollywood actresses came to see them fight. Mae West came to watch regularly and wrote about the desire of 'soft female bodies' to be 'touched' by the 'raw irritated flesh which had been scraped on the ring ropes.' This thrill might not work the same way for women. There are female boxers who wear lace for weigh-ins. Women's boxing has got glamorous because it is making more money. They are better promoted, and because of this, they are made more beautiful. They are strong, marketable—above all they are good. They are objects of desire too.

The girls who have boxed before in this gym say I'll need all my hair back; braids work best because nothing can flip in front of your eyeline. I don't want to wear shorts. It feels silly, at my age. I think I will wear leggings, a vest. I don't know if I should show my stomach or not. If that softest part of my female body is something I want exposed. But there is a part of me tempted to show myself off in this solid and strongest form. There is muscle there, in my stomach.

My trainer looks pleased, proud.

'I didn't know you were going to be that tough. I didn't know you were going to be able to take a hit.'

I hug this woman. Her name is Donna. I feel high. Wired. I feel I could do it all again. We plan to do it again—she tells me it's hard to find women to spar with now. She has to use men, because of height and power. I look at my face in the mirror, it's red where I've been hit, blotchy, a little puffy, my hair roughed up by her gloves—static and sweat. I am a mess. My nose begins to bang. But I feel good.

We watch it back on video and I'm surprised to see my body so sure of itself. It doesn't match the pain I'm starting to feel. On screen I look free, as if I am enjoying it. I am not self-conscious, I bounce, I hunch, I am not the same woman who walks down the street playing with my hair or crossing my legs to slim my body on the tube. I am big. I skip around the parameters of the ring and fill its centre.

I see the moment where I get knocked. It's a second of shock, my head nudged, then I am back, guard up. My trainer gives me water. 'You're going to be fine. I'm not worried about you at all.' This is why he is so good for me. He tells me everything is going to be okay.

I get myself a coffee on the way home from the café across the road, my hand still wrapped, the blood still there in its small, triumphant stain.

6

The cups of tea would always get cold. She would fall sleep before she could drink them, hands balanced on her protruding, swollen stomach. Her veins ropey, the blood scratching its way around her body—all effort. Just a slip of skin and limb, the T-shirts I took in for her swallowed her small frame like Roman robes. I remove her wedding ring and keep it in a wooden box, in case it slips from her finger. My dad read her poetry, reciting from Seamus Heaney's District and Circle *as she slept, or woke—there was always little difference between the two. She would never be fully awake for long before the blackout of morphine sleep. She would ask me to go on an errand for her. The same every afternoon—to get a gooseberry yoghurt from the Sainsbury's across the main road. I always returned with two because it felt like exactly the time to be giving more than what she'd asked, and I'd put one of them in her fridge. She would feed herself. Taking the plastic spoon and moving it to her mouth as her left wrist pushed the nose feed to the side. After she ate half, she stared at the space ahead, arranging her hands, before picking up her notepad, slowly, with difficulty, to write her to-do list. She wanted to make sure the laundry got done. She is worried about Dad. She wants to make sure he knows how to do an online shop. That he should get a cleaner to help him around the house.*

I go home after my first spar and sit at the table, catching up with work.

The world feels quiet. The fuss and thrill of sparring—of all the cortisol and adrenalin—is over. I slump. I haven't felt a fatigue like this before. It's sudden. I am typing and then my eyes burn, my neck cannot hold my head. I need to lie down. I have two hours before I collect my daughter and the exhaustion hurts.

I want a bath, but this will make it worse, so I have a coffee, tapping at the bridge of my nose in a mindful, careful way. The pain waking me up. Already I feel like I have a cold. I message the younger trainer I always talk to. He calms and soothes. He says this is normal after a spar. He tells me to remember I have changed my whole nervous system. This helps me understand this might be much more about my body than my mind and I try to let the tiredness be something that can soothe me.

I am making a support network. I have become good at doing this as a single mother. I find people and places to act as community for me and my daughter. Men are still new to me. But boxing has become a way of assembling the kind I want in my life. I am putting a world back together, reshaping the scaffolds of a life that lost its centre. I feel nurtured. I don't find their machismo brittle or threatening. They welcome my body, my ideas. They celebrate me, and the other women here. They get me to play to my strengths—my grace, lightness—to dance in the ring, to tell stories. So far, these are uncomplicated relationships. So far, the idea of sex hasn't got in our way. The boxers are exactly what I need and when we speak about my body, we speak about it like we would a machine, a weapon. It's exciting to talk about myself like this. Strength and speed are power. I am complimented on the quickness of my jab. How long my arms are. My body as anatomic and useful.

Instead of a bath I fill the sink and hold a warm flannel to my face, wiping away the last crust of blood. I sniff into the swelling, and I massage rose oil into any tenderness. Under the eyes and in between my fingers. I want to feel creamy and pretty again, softened, back to myself. My left eye is bloodshot. A dark shadow already forming. I look bad, but I am fascinated too, in this changing appearance. How quickly a face can be altered.

The oil soaks into my skin quickly. I apply make-up. A quick flick of mascara over eyes that feel dead and heavy. I file and paint my nails. As if being hit never happened at all. The only sign it happened is my blocked right nostril where the cartilage has bruised. I have another two coffees to wake up and as I walk to school, I call my dad. He is against this. He asks me if I realise what this could do to me—the damage it could cause. He was there when I used to cause myself harm—the one to take me to hospitals. He would wait up at the kitchen table with Mum, sometimes without her. Making tea and putting a record on.

'Get to bed.' Never telling me off. Just ushering me back to safety.

He doesn't understand boxing. He doesn't get the need to fight with hands and has only had a few instances where he's been hurt. A broken knee from rugby, a football scar on his shin. He tells me he can't get his head around it, why I'd want to be in pain. But he doesn't stop me or try to. He takes his role as lone parent seriously and checks in with me every day now Mum is gone. He lives in the countryside, where we cared for Mum, and I call to tell him about the nosebleed. Later, he writes his spare little message... Concussion? I call him back and say the bleed was light, minor—it was nothing. It occurs to me as I walk that he will sit there, alone in the house he shared with Mum, thinking of my nosebleed, and if I'm going to be okay.

He has seen enough. He also cleaned her sores, felt unsettled by her laboured, stressed breathing. Watched her body fade in his hands.

'Are you sure you want to do this?'

I ignore the question and instead turn to my daughter's father. He gets it. He grew up fighting. It feels the right thing to do, especially as there will be times and moments where I carry a bruise she can see. I need him to reassure her with me.

I need him for advice, for care. I tell him about the first nosebleed, and he tells me how good it is for me. He says I can't hit someone until I've been hit properly. He believes this and refers to his own childhood. He was there when Mum died, saw my nipple crust over when I breastfed—has checked my stitches after birth. He knows my body. He has helped to fix my body before. He has also hurt me.

He says it is good for me to learn I can get hurt, and it is not the end. Instead of feeling sorry for me he asks...
'But did it hurt, really?'

I consider. I thought it did, but he is right, it aches, I feel it. But it isn't that bad.

'Did it hurt, or did she just catch you in the right place, made your eyes water?'

There was blood, but not for long. I wiped it away and it was gone. He is right. It didn't hurt, really.

When I see my daughter, it reminds me of my own softness. I hold her and tell her I love her. We go for pizza before her ballet class and I ignore my headache and drink water, listening to her tell me about the silly things the boys at her table say. She isn't amused by them. She tells me they just talk about snakes and poison. I know she does probably find it funny, because she smiles as she speaks, and as I brush and twist her hair into a perfect ballet bun, with net and clips, I admire her lovely neck and the curls that whisper at its nape. She has a beauty spot on her ear, and I kiss it. She smells of the conditioning spray—of coconut and the sweet sweat of her day.

I drop her off and sit in my usual Moroccan bakery and drink mint tea.

I think of myself punching into air and space. I wonder what I'm doing this for. Then I see a message from my trainer... You were great. He says little in messages, but it is just enough. It always counts. My mood lifts.

It's cold outside. I haven't eaten enough. I'm still learning how to treat myself better. As I work through this new violent streak, I'm understanding I need to look after myself. When we are home, I make myself a proper meal. It is hot, full of carbohydrates and cream and it is delicious. I feel better. We eat at the table together, my daughter and I, both of us tired and hungry. The pasta fills us, and we are warm, fed. I will not skip meals. I will not treat myself as if I don't need to be well. I will not live as if I can live on nothing.

I go to bed at the same time as my daughter. I close my eyes and sleep all the way through until 3 a.m., waking in darkness. I remember I have said yes to the fight. How outside of my comfort zone this is, to be so vulnerable, again and again, and how essential that is for me to move. The worst is over, watching Mum leave the world. To never have her again. I fall back to sleep, hunting jawlines with jabs—practicing hooks that land on nobody.

7

I go to see Mum in the afternoon. She is awake, smiling. She has some energy and asks me to give her a wash. It has to be done carefully, otherwise it hurts and burns. Even running water feels like weight. I ask the nurse how to work around her feed and tubes and she gives me a little pack with a cap I can microwave. When I put it on Mum's head I press lightly and lather with a special soap. I rinse the same way—with a plastic cap. Mum bends her head low so I can fit it over her hair. I have to be so gentle; I have to be so careful. I rub as if I was washing a newborn, small, tender circles and she holds a thumb and finger to my wrist, for comfort, and also for control— so she might be able to slow me down if I hurt her. She closes her eyes, and I feel like her mother. I brush and braid her hair, which she has still kept, despite being blasted by all kinds of treatment. A ribbon of grey at the front. I have bought her a face oil—a rose oil—and I circle it into her skin as if I am blotting tissue, then into her arms and legs. She is so dry, so sore. I rub the oil into her heels and arches, and she begins to doze into sleep. She is smiling, in a pillow of light. 'Thank you,' she says, as if I have done her a favour. And all I have done is rub roses into her skin.

The second spar is different to the first. Again, it's with a woman. She has had a lot more experience—a lot more fights.

Liv reminds me to remove my earrings. I quietly react against it, as if she is telling me what to do. As if we are still in school. I have to remember she is trying to help me. Sparring, I have to remember, isn't a fight. It is rehearsal and growth. I'm supposed to learn. It's feeling out space and hurt.

I am more confident now. I am learning to go slower, to feel my way through pauses and breath. I try to create that space and time for myself. Every so often I hear my trainer bark that there is a minute to go—then 30 seconds to go. Then it's 10—and these last seconds always feel like the longest. I circle her, and she moves back. I keep jabbing. Pushing her back, pushing her away. Not too hard, just touches, like fencing, to her head, her neck. I have long arms. It works for me. If I can create range, I can dictate the tempo of each round. Liv knows this, and she cuts me off. She knows how to defend, and she has ideas. This comes from experience. Although I manage a big jab between her eyes, she manages to hit me more. There is one moment I punch to her head, the first time I have managed to do it—up until now I have been too afraid to hurt her—and when I do, she calls out, 'nice!' in a kind of solidarity—passing on confidence, praise. Then in the last round she hits me hard. She lets her hands go. I am bad at defending myself, I don't get my head out of the way in time. I leave myself open, on the line, for these types of punches. I hear voices telling me to angle off.

But it doesn't matter. I have improved, and we hug after. The intensity of those three rounds creates real intimacy and we feel like friends. We talk about periods. How to fight when you're bleeding.

'Think of all the other things you can do on a period. This is just another thing.'

I get advice on my skin—told to expect spots, even acne. 'Remember my gloves are hitting other faces, the germs can spread.'

There is something like school about it. The way girls create their own rooms and circles in hushed conversation about the body. It is like being in the girl's toilets. 'Be prepared for bad skin.'

When I go through the video with my trainer I watch and learn again. I am not stepping into my punches. I'm not spiteful enough. I feel the suddenness of tears and begin to cry. I can't explain it, only that I have been disturbed by this fight and my body is reacting to it. My trainer looks uncomfortable—he says he can't do crying—but he hugs me anyway. I need this physical care too, after being hit, my body needs comfort. I need a mother. When I cry another male fighter steps into the ring to tell me that sometimes he feels like crying too, but never does. We begin a whole conversation about the need for tears. They are nothing to do with our sadness. It's the response to fighting. I wonder if they would allow themselves this conversation, these soldiers and fighters, if I wasn't here. If I hadn't cried.

That night I cleanse my face twice. The bruise comes up quickly. A brown stripe across the bridge of my nose and into the socket of my left eye. A small map, turning the colour of smoke and ash. This one hurts. Much more than it did in its moment. My body keeps stepping into these punches. Too readily—with too much ease. They are mistakes, but they are obvious ones I need to fix. I have to move my head. I need to get out of the way. I rub arnica on the bruising. It is tender.

My daughter returns home with her dad. They both look at my face. He smiles, she stares at me as if I'm not quite her mother.

'Was that from boxing?'

My daughter's dad nods—he's become sage-like about these things. It's the only way you'll know how to get hit—when you get hit yourself.

He gets the peas out of the freezer and holds them to my face in a tea towel.

'You'll feel tired. Expect to feel tired.' He is soft with me; he knows about this. He's been hit enough times. He understands how to heal after being hit hard.

'Remember, you're asking your body to fight. It's primal. You're getting into deep layers.'

His nose has been changed forever through fighting. This is the nicest he has ever been to me. We have met somewhere—a shared language. He has become my friend.

The next morning, I go to the shops across the road to get milk and coffee and there is a man by the counter staring. Others glance and then look again. Men and women. When I get home and look in the mirror the bruise has darkened again—like the undead—a charcoal. My eyes sunken. I look unwell—I look like I have been punched.

I want to announce it—a woman did this to me, not a man. I am not that statistic. I asked for this, I was boxing. This was supposed to happen.

It is isolating, this world, if there is no one to talk to about it. Most of my friends don't box and wouldn't. To do this to yourself is extreme and I don't know why I am. Except I know my history, the relationship I have had to my body and to pain. And the way I used to harm myself for a small window in my early twenties. When I found myself in the corner of a kitchen watching blood pop from small cuts on my arm. Mum dabbing with warm salt water. I would be breathless, and she would sit with me on the floor, until I had stopped shaking. When the worst was over, she'd make tea with honey and time slowed and I was myself again, looking down at my arm in disgust, with regret. Apologising to Mum who was always so good at making it seem as if it was all going to be fixed in time.

'It'll fade, we will get the sun on it.'

This was her favourite thing to say about all our wounds, all our hurt. To join her outside, to sit in the sun. It came from Grandad. He insisted on us sitting on chairs by his rockery, sprouting lavender, the pot of tea on a tray in the grass. It was always better to be outside if it was warm enough. When Mum was in her last weeks of life, I still thought the sunlight would keep her with me for longer.

I can never forgive myself for letting her see my arms. How she must have felt when she'd gone back to bed, after making sure I fell asleep, her hand on my forehead, a gentle pressure to let me know she was there. I couldn't explain it. I could only tell her that it was an anger I didn't have words for. Her thumb stroking the skin between my eyes, hushing me if the tears came again. Telling me we would find a way to understand it.

I think about this, as I treat my nose with more arnica, that maybe I am still in that place. Except I don't feel shame, and I don't feel out of control. Everything in the ring was composed. I had to show patience, skill—I had to play chess with my opponent. It begins a conversation with my body that I haven't yet been able to have, because at the same time as being injured,

I am growing stronger. My arms, more sculpted. My stomach hard. I have stopped drinking, and my sleep is better, perhaps because of deep exhaustion, I sleep through the night, waking with headache and thirst, but the sleep itself is uninterrupted.

I am practicing how to be aggressive. Each time I have sparred I am showing my body it's okay to attack, to come forward. This begins to play out into my life. I notice I have less patience with colleagues, friends, and strangers. At the moment I don't want to invite anyone to my fight. I don't want to tell anyone about it yet. I can imagine the responses, the confusion.

My moods shift and I find myself withdrawn, quiet, I don't want to put myself in places where there is alcohol, so I turn down invites. I am enjoying this clean, solid body, but I feel alone and isolated by it too. It would be an easier life to smoke and drink and laugh. When I am not boxing, or training, I am waiting until I can do it again. There is a vein in my left bicep. I notice it when I am in plank, prominent when my arm is tense. There is a cut on the knuckle of my little finger I have to wrap in plasters, an open wound from punching. The small, deep gash taking forever to heal because I keep opening it up on the punchbag.

This gym is becoming the place I feel most at home in. It is a culture, a family. I miss it when I'm not there. The mother I can't have. The witness to my pain and healing. To hold the tissue when I have my nosebleed. This is my world now. These men are healing me.

8

On my visits I watched her sleep. Just to look at the way her body tried to untangle breath. Under the brute pallor of yellow, hospital light, her chest had blotted into patches of shadow, as if the pain had eclipsed skin and created a darkness. It rose and fell, and I counted each time I heard air moaning from her mouth.

When I get home, I listen to the message from my trainer asking if I can come to the gym the next morning. He's set up a special spar for me. He doesn't say who it's with. It is less personal that way. When you get invited to spar, even if it's last minute, you try and make it happen. Getting the right girls in the ring at the same time isn't easy. I cancel meetings to make it work—moving things around to make sure these 20 minutes can happen.

There is now a ritual to getting ready. I wear black. All my clothes for boxing are black. I have a lot of hair—heavy as a sack—and if I don't scrape it back it gets in the way. I can't see what I'm doing.

I pull it all back into a ponytail and then braid it into a long, thick plait.I pack my mouthguard, gloves, and put a plaster around the finger that keeps bleeding at the knuckles. It never stops it stinging—even when I wrap three thick plasters around the wound.

I never forget breakfast. I used to. I'd think nothing of leaving the house with only coffee in my stomach. But there is a need for it now. I can't do the rounds without food. Boxing returns me to the fundamentals, the basics. I boil my egg and then, when I have eaten and packed, I rub rose oil over my arms, my neck, and hands. It is a final kind of counter to the assault of getting hit, scraped, and grazed. As if the oil will act as a barrier—a shield. A final feminine foil. It's the same rose oil I used on my mum's skin when she was parched. It is the exact same bottle.

And then the hand wraps. It has taken me a long time to understand how to put them on. My trainer used to do them for me, but since starting camp I feel a responsibility to learn— to grow up. It feels proper, adult.

It's ceremonial. It takes me time. A meditation. I do the left hand first, three times around my thin wrist, winding into the thumb and around the side of the hand. I twist and weave like my grandmother did on her loom. Until I am padded and protected and bound. I open and close my fist to make sure I have room—that it won't suffocate in the glove. I need to be able to make a fist.

I head to the station and start to feel the familiar sickness and thrill of walking to have a spar. The potency of that particular fear and excitement.

I walk into the gym and already my trainer is there, in the ring. He barks at me, as always.

'What time do you call this?'

Even though I am on time. There are three other women in the ring. One is Donna—she looks easy and relaxed, finishing her energy bar and sipping water. The other two I know, but I don't know them well. They are supposed to be fighting too—and technically in camp, like me. All three of us look anxious. This jump into the intimacy of belting each other in the face and round the head needs a kind of fortitude—a courage—it's a skill.

The idea is this—we will do two rounds with each girl swapping each time, until we have all met each other in the ring. We will each have rest; each have two rounds with the other.

It turns out we all have a PhD.

'You ever seen three boxer-doctors before.'

There is laughter. A small crowd is here, watching the fight. Spars are exciting to watch. You can see the mistakes—the dress rehearsal. The moves that are tried and tested.

But it's the first time I've had to do this in front of a crowd, and something shifts. I'm aware of being looked at. Of not looking stupid. I feel there is less room for mistakes. Some of the men watching are boxers.

We laugh too, looking at each other, not for support, but as each other's witness, but it's a nervous laugh.

The first is technically better than me, but I am taller, and I use my length, my space. She lands some nice shots to the body, but because I can create so much space between the two of us, they don't hurt and I keep circling and jabbing, my left arm landing to her head. Something else too—I am happier to hit her and get hit. She punches light—I don't feel them. And she looks scared to be there. It feels suddenly odd to be the one making someone else hurt. The two spars I've had so far have taught me big lessons in how to receive pain—taking a punch to the face isn't something you learn to do—you can do it, or you can't. She quickly becomes my opponent—the other—and I stalk her. I don't mind hurting her at all.

Eventually our two minutes is up. She rests in her corner, and I go straight into fighting the other doctor.

She is even smaller and comes at me with more aggression. She charges at me, throwing right hands and I keep her off, my jab acting as my defence. She can't get to me. I throw one-twos and keep her in corners. But then she buttons me. Her right hand finds that little gap and she's landed so hard on my jaw I feel rattled. I swing for her. My impulse is to take her head off too. I throw a lopping right hand to the side of her body instead.

'Right. Both of you ten press-ups now.'

There is too much heat.

'It's not meant to be a war.'

We both laugh. But something has been altered. A kind of agreement broken. I take it personally, what she just did. If I wasn't in so much pain, I'd have a temper. We go back to our corners, and I need to sit down. It feels as if my teeth have been rearranged in my jaw, I can't bite down properly—it feels as if my back molars have been taken out. I begin to dislike her for a second and look at her with playground hate. I know the rules of sparring. You aren't supposed to try and take each others' heads off. I sit with my jaw in my hand, trying to feel if there's a break. My tongue feels loose.

One of the older boxers notices I'm in pain and comes over to me, putting my jaw in his hands. He cups my face like he's weighing it—as if his palms are the scales.

'It isn't broken. You'd know if it was broken.'

His hands are rough. But I appreciate the touch. Being hurt

this way is a shock and being held feels like I'm being put back together.

'You're okay.'

But the bones on the left side of my face feel crushed, collapsed. I keep opening and shutting my mouth to rewire it back to centre, as if it has springs and I can make them work again, simply by moving my mouth. It doesn't worry me, but the pain softens, and the girl steps out of the ring, shaking her hair out of the headguard. This irritates me too. I wasn't wearing one.

I go up to her.

'That was the hardest anyone has ever hit me.'

She looks nervous, embarrassed about it. I give her a hug.

'I practiced that a lot in training,' she tells me.

'It worked.'

I am smiling. I respect her. But it hurts.

My trainer is looking for me from his corner.

'Want to sit the last round out?'

I think about it, the last round is against Donna. I need to find a way to work through pain, defeat, so I step back in the ring.

When I was 12 my mum and grandad found the money to pay for me to go to Pony Club—and I was good at it. A natural rider. I didn't have my own horse, but a woman we knew gave me the horses from her stable who weren't fully trained or had some trauma in their background. They'd been beaten, or frightened. Left alone until their hooves curled and their manes knotted. She rescued them. Or she bought them cheap. They were bad on roads and afraid of other horses—or couldn't jump. They were useless in shows. On one cross-country competition I had to ride the pony who halted on every jump, and I got thrown off each time. I'd gather him up, squeezing with my thighs, kicking, and moving my body to encourage him to take his front legs off the ground. I'd coax and pull and kick and soothe and every time he would buck me off. I'd fall, usually on my side, and get back on, silently, without crying. I was 14 and used to it. Eventually, after falling several times I led him around the course. We walked to the finish line together, hopeless, dishevelled, my hair falling from its net—the pony scalloped in clumped mud. It was sobering, tiresome. But it was never a humiliation. The judges knew a scared horse wasn't going to jump. But we had to finish because otherwise we'd come nowhere at all.

My mum signed me up to make me feel I could mix it with posh girls and hold my own. My grandad pushed for it too. They wanted this on my CV. They wanted this to be something I felt entitled to.

I nod to my trainer and put my mouthguard back in. My gloves are back on.

He inspects me. He feels the side of my jaw.

'You good?'

I nod again.

'Just focus on not getting hit. She won't take the piss with you. She's good.'

It's the only reason I'm doing this. Donna wants me to get better, not to beat me up. We pace around and circle each other, and she throws neat, clean shots at my body and head to make me move.

'Move your head,' she hisses. 'Go on, move your head.' Irritated almost, that I'm so static.

The boxers watching join in too. They cheer when I get out of the way. When I land a jab they clap... 'Yes, Anna.' Not to side against Donna, but to encourage me. To give me the confidence they think I need.

I get out of her way. A couple land but we finish the two

minutes and I'm relieved. My jaw bangs and Donna hugs me. She is barely out of breath.

'That girl before me... she was throwing too hard. Put a bag of peas on it.'

I thank her.

I leave without saying goodbye. It's a sulk. I just about wave a hand, but I want to leave.

The punch lingers. It crawls along the side of my face, still lashing at nerve endings. I order a smoothie for lunch, sipping on the straw with my slack, loose mouth, and fighting back tears. I call my ex, my daughter's father.

'I've had that. Go and sleep and take two paracetamols.'

He doesn't dwell on pain for too long. Mine, or his.

'She caught you right. Those shots hurt.'

For him, pain is fact. It isn't something up for discussion.

He says he will get our daughter from school which means I can rest. I begin to feel the chill that comes with shock and walk slowly to the train station, arms folded. It's becoming hard to do this alone. I'm still wearing the wraps. I undo the Velcro with my teeth to unwind them and the pain courses through my cheek again. I really feel the skull beneath the skin—my flesh as something that can fall apart. On the Hammersmith and City line, for those four stops back home, I feel unsure of all this.

9

Mum was getting worried that they were making her change rooms for no reason and messaged me when I was on the train to London to teach a class. She understood this moving as a total chaos. She was anxious about having to use a new bathroom, even though the one she'd be using would be private. She was insulted—that they thought she could just be moved at all. We all knew she'd be moving to a hospice soon and in a way this didn't matter. But it did to her. She was losing control of her life. I told her that a private bathroom would be better for her in the long run. But she knew there was no long run. That there was only now. Only these moments of panic.

I continue to teach around my boxing training. Every Friday I teach my undergraduates about masculinity, a course I developed myself. We look at male characters in literature. How heroes change over time.

The recent spar has given me a prominent bruise above my left eye—a print of ink by the lid. And a blue strip across my nose that looks like tribal make-up.

I don't try to cover it up. I don't see the point—these bruises have been earned and I'm happy to have them. There is no shame. I almost want to be asked about them.

I walk into my class, and most are there. It's mostly young women. We are working through the film adaptation of Alan Sillitoe's novel, *Saturday Night, and Sunday Morning*, discussing the fight scene at the beginning. Arthur, played by a handsome Albert Finney rolls down the stairs, drunk. They find the main character tedious, offensive—but over the next hour they warm to him. 'It's the writing,' they say. 'The writer knows he's tragic. He lets us feel sorry for him.'

One of the more confident girls in the room asks me what happened to my face. I tell them I'm getting ready for my first fight. There is a mix of surprise, some giggling. Embarrassed for me, maybe.

'But why? I don't get why anyone likes boxing.'

And then the question that feels important, given I'm teaching a course about the ways women can get hurt through male violence.

'Aren't women hurt enough—why would you put yourself in the ring?'

I feel an obligation to explain. They are my students. They are young women—and I am also a mother.

'Does it hurt?'

I tell them yes.

'It hurts like being hit is supposed to hurt. But I am also hurting back.'

They don't like that it's women hitting each other.

I explain that all the reasons they have for not liking it are the same reasons I love doing it. There is no justification with boxing. It is violent. I say the thing my trainer says to me... 'You have to get hit.'

Then I reassure them.

'But there is also something in watching your face heal. There is power in watching your body know what to do.'

I tell them to put their books down for a moment. I pause the reading and instead turn on the screen in the seminar room and load up one of Mikaela Mayer's first fights against the boxer Maïva Hamadouche. It's well-known for being a tear-up with both women hammering away at the other, heads rocking, Mayer wielding her right hand up like an axe.

I show them this fight because of the entrance. It is the way Mayer walks into the ring that captivates the girls in my class.

There is a live electric guitar, the female guitarist from Alice Cooper. Mayer emerges in a silk robe, hood up over her eyes so you can hardly see her stare. Just the lines of her jaw—the fists in gloves at her sides. She is breathtaking. Some girls gasp—she silences them.

'But she's so beautiful. Are boxers supposed to be this beautiful.'

A girl at the back of the class is captivated.

I pause the fight when the two women meet in the middle of the ring.

'Who do you think wins this?'

Mayer's stillness convinces them. But I think in this story, where one of the two must be the winner, it is her beauty that charms them too. They want her to be the winner.

'Mayer wins this.'

I nod.

'She does.'

They say I have spoiled the ending.

And even the ones who don't want to box, or like boxing, look disappointed that I jumped to the end too soon.

'You need to know the result. I want you to all study the first round and tell me who looks like they're more in control.'

The fight is close in the first round—and both fighters come in with aggression. But it's Mayer's height—her body that looks the most powerful. She stalks her opponent with a grace and an anger, constantly pushing and pressing and throwing lefts and rights like the swell in a wave—muscle in water. It flows, easy, and it belts the face of Hamadouche.

It helps that Mayer is beautiful. That she is legs and cheekbones—gold sweat.

But she is also the better fighter.

'It just felt so relentless. I didn't expect the fight to be that aggressive.'

They beg to watch until the end, but we need to finish the book.

I compromise.

'Write about what you saw. For next week—try describing it.'

I leave on time and run to the station to make the train to get my daughter. I wonder if I should have showed them a boxing clip. If it was appropriate content. If any of the girls in my class might find that hard. But the following week each one has written up their pages and when they are read out, they are all excellent—savage and beautiful and poetic.

I tell my dad. He doesn't like boxing. Refuses to watch my fight.

'You can't expect people to love it like you do. You have to expect this—a lot of people don't like it.'

I snap at him. I jump to boxing's defence.

'But they should.'

He is calm, composed. My dad never liked fighting. Can't understand my need to do it. He lets me shout at him and says, with quiet power... 'Anna, you have to be able to have that discussion.'

10

The feed wasn't going to work. There wasn't enough body for it to attach to. Her skin, crepe and always black and blueish, was too flimsy to hold a needle, let alone withstand any surgery. She was barely flesh against her skeleton. And everything hurt: the shower, the toilet, the moving of a mattress. I was watching her, fading to ash—to where she would be lost— vanishing to white.

When they sat down to hold her hand and tell her it wouldn't be possible, that there was nothing more to be done, she smiled. She didn't want the doctor to feel bad.

'Not to worry,' she spoke in calm. Tapping her thumb slowly onto theirs. 'We'll make do.'

Her brain not really hers anymore. Just partial—fractal—pieces of her story, moving into that whiteness.

I wanted the feed stitched into her. Just because it was a thing that would keep her connected to us. To this world we wanted her to belong to.

I have left Sylvie with my dad to come here tonight and watch sparring, and for the first time I'm dressed in things I don't box in. A blazer, jeans—I am in make-up too. I choose the most awkward place to sit—edging as far away from the ring as I can. I perch at the edge of a running machine, with only a narrow space for a seat, so that my knees are drawn together at an angle and my hands rest on them, clutching, unnatural. I wait to be noticed. It is usually a glance, or a longer stare before the eyes go back to the bag, or the pads, or the trainer. No one is supposed to sleep with each other— at least not so anyone finds out.

'She's educated,' my trainer tells anyone. As if this is the thing that keeps me apart—some arbitrary idea of an education.

I appreciate it. He wants me to focus on boxing. To not get myself distracted, stuck in tensions and dramas. He also knows the history—he knows about the trysts and flings inside this gym. He wants me to take myself seriously.

When new boxers come into the gym to catch up with him on their fights, their plan—their conditioning—they glance at me and before they can size me up my trainer makes my announcement...

'This is Anna. She's good. She's quite good.' And he is messing with me—and them.

Sometimes he goes into detail... 'She's got a brilliant jab.'

There is a difference between men and women in boxing. I've seen it. The boys hit harder. I have seen the power in the way men throw. The crack and crunch when the gloves find the target. The way chains rattle on heavy bags when they throw a hook. The women hit hard too—but the men hit harder.

The gym is small. We quickly become characters—recognising each other in a lunchtime circuit, or like this evening, a night of sparring.

The names need to be drawn from a hat and I get asked to pick them out. It's for fairness. I am embarrassed—I have to stand up and limp with my dead leg—slowly, dramatically, to the ring. As a relatively new face I am not known to everyone, and the men ask my name. The man in charge, muscled, tanned, stocky—turns only slightly to me. As if my name doesn't matter. I tell them who I am. I pick out the names they need, holding the folded paper in the palm of my hand. Name by name the evening is arranged. The man in charge starts to call them out and before he does, he turns to me and says thank you—but asks my name again. In a deliberate and laboured way. I find myself repeating it for the third time, my voice cold, young, and not my own. As if to beg him—please remember who I am.

The sparring happens. The men take their place in the ring and go the three rounds. I watch each one—the heat, the skill, the fury. But I am distracted. It was the way the man refereeing the rounds made me say my name twice. It's not quite shame, but I feel as if I wasn't enough. Not enough to be remembered the first time.

I want to leave but am here and have to stick out the rest of the evening. I play with my hair and return to old behaviours. I find angles for my body to move in, crossing legs again, putting on lipstick—pouting, with my own fury. I force my sex. I want to be the one they admire.

I cross and uncross my legs again.

But I am not the focus. And as the rain cracks outside and the heat rises inside, and the men snap and jab and belt each other in the side, stomach and head, I sit in my quiet, wishing they'd know my name. I want them to see me. Know my name, I want to say. I want to tell them again, what my name is.

I need to spar—I need to be in that ring. No one cares unless you're here to fight. You have to earn a name.

II

Mum is moved to the hospice. I can't make it back for the move.
I am working. I hear from my sister that it's nice, peaceful. That
it's a place to accept that the ending is definite. This is the start
of the real ending. The hospital was knotty uncertainty—but this
will be the place she dies in. There is supposed to be comfort in
this. Perhaps she can finally relax, knowing she won't have to pack
her bags again. I book a meeting with the priest who tells me she is
preparing for her place in eternity.

I am going to get hurt.

I have been sparring once or twice a week—it has been
challenging, but I'm not getting beaten up too badly. That hasn't
happened yet. The odd bloody nose. The bruised lid of an eye.

This week I am set up against a girl I've heard about—she is
bigger than me, has boxed for years. She is the best female boxer
from this gym. There are posters of her fights on the wall.

There is energy to this spar—it's been building, growing—we are two of the tallest women from this gym—it attracts attention. A crowd watches. The gym is fuller than usual. It's a compliment that this is something worth watching, but it comes with real fear. As I walk in I feel it, I know the outcome of this will be a brutal one. I am going to get hurt today.

My hair is in its high ponytail and braided, and, as ever, I am in black. The woman I am going to spar asks if I want any Vaseline and I say no—I have never used it before and I don't see why I should start using it now.

'Why do you need it?'

She is smearing it beneath and over her eye, with the precision of someone who knows what they're doing. A professional.

'Because it stops the marks.'

I shake my head. I'm hostile to it. I don't want her help—just like when the other girls told me to tie my hair back or take my earrings off—I find taking advice from other women difficult. Clearly, she knows more than I do—has done this more times than me. And so, I resist her help—I do it my way. I shake my head because I don't want to do what I'm told. She fills out the ring in a way I don't. She is used to this—to being the winner. I can see her confidence. I turn to my corner—my trainer is watching but can't do my corner because of any perceived favouritism—so I have a young, very well-spoken boxer, who seems nice. He tells me I need to make angles. This means creating spaces for punching. Throwing punches is easy—but they need to land. They need to make contact, to cause some damage. Making angles and shifting space. The more I spar, the more technical it becomes.

Very quickly, I realise how good she is. Until this spar I have been meeting shorter girls in the ring. I have been able to use my jab to keep them away—at a literal arm's length. I have long arms and this, if I am honest and smug, has made my life easier. My arms have hung at my sides, I've been able to step back and find range—I have used my space in the ring. There have been nasty and powerful right hands to my head, but my height has kept these away most of the time.

There have been tough spars, but this, within seconds, is clearly the toughest so far. The woman whips her jab into my face, and I am applauded and admired for taking the punch. I know what this means—she landed hard—and I didn't fall, or collapse. I feel it in a way I haven't felt a punch before. A sharp, brutal pain between the eyes that makes me pause, but I know I have to keep going. I am relieved when the round ends and I don't know how I am going to survive the next two.

The boy in my corner smiles and says I'm doing well, in that way that makes me think I'm not doing well at all. I am breathing heavily, but I go back out, to the centre of the ring. We touch gloves. I hear my trainer telling me to step back. To stick my jab. To keep sticking my jab.

But she is so strong. She uses her height in a way I haven't learned how to—not yet. I get moved into corners and twist and shift my way out. Her punches land hard. I move from a few, but I realise I'm taking more punches than I ever have. I throw some too. Some even land. But this is a one-sided show, and I'm taking the big hits.

I have a final round to get through. And I don't know how I am going to move. My face stings.

I go back out and meet her in the middle of the ring again. She throws jabs so quickly, I try to block and move my head, but I keep getting caught. For the final minute I see mist and walk into them, throwing as I go, hoping some land, willing the seconds to finish. I hear someone call out '15 seconds' and I count them. Time moves smashed and scattered. I, the both of us, are moving through this last bit, baiting the other, seeing who will get the last punch. It's me. I think it's me. I don't know, but I think I get the last body shot. It doesn't matter. My face is hot with pain.

My trainer calls it out... 'She got the better of you, but you held your own.'

He says this to make me feel better, but there is truth in it too. I did. I tried.

I step out of the ring and everyone who watched the spar pats my back, shakes my hand. Sparring this woman is a big deal. I smile and say thank you. Some of the girls stare at me.

I look at myself in the mirror. I try to wipe away the mascara that has bled out. Then I remember I didn't put mascara on, and this is the start of a strange new bruise. The area above my eyes is spattered—with inky stripes and dots. I keep thinking it's make-up, but I'm not wearing any. I keep wiping, robotically, as if it's going to rub off.

'Annabella are you okay.'

Another coach comes over to me.

'I'm fine, really I'm fine.' I smile. I don't want anyone to feel sorry for me.

And then the woman I sparred comes over too and tells me she is sorry. This somehow makes it worse.

'I didn't want to hit you like that, they told me to put it on you. To get you ready for the fight.'

I hug her and tell her it is what I wanted. There isn't a mark on her face.

I back onto the running machine behind me and tell them

both I am going to go for a quick 15 minute run to get rid of the energy. I start jogging, and my eyes purple as I do. I've never seen this kind of transformation happen so quickly—my features fatten and darken, like rotting fruit. The bruises case each eye, my nose flames in pain and swells, fat. I run and watch my face become someone else's face—it is as if a monster is seeping to the skin. There are scales and stripes and blood spots I haven't seen before. After ten minutes I stop the machine and head to the door—I wave behind me, my face in my hands. I am ashamed, and I am in pain. I take my bag and put my hood up and walk out, taking a wrong turn. I am confused, lost. I find my way again and want to hide. The tears come as soon as I am out of the alley way, heading for the station. I don't mind strangers looking, but I didn't want the gym to see.

When I am home, I take a photo of my face, my nose not only larger, but hooked, as if the cartilage has been yanked. All I seem to do is watch my face become another face. Touching my nose to check for the places that hurt. I send the photos to my trainer. I want it to be seen—witnessed. He tells me I did great. I send the same photo to my daughter's father. He is shocked. But he tells me I'd know if my nose was broken.

'Trust me, you'd be howling.'

I believe him. In all things that are violent, I believe him.

But the pain feels so smudged, so all over, so a part of me now, that I don't know how to split it. I should have put Vaseline around my eyes. I can't even wash, I am not tired, I just hurt. These two things aren't the same, I realise. I lie on my bed, eyes open, waiting to feel the pulse and beat of each hit through my body as something I can learn to ride—breathe in to. It is not the same, but it is similar to the way I gave birth in my mother's bed. The contractions thumping into tender spaces and my arms grabbing the bed post to steady my thrashing and twisting body.

These punches sting. I can't breathe—I can't cry. I do wonder how much more my body can understand about this new language of pain.

12

My sister is here. It makes a big difference, to share this burden. To split the sadness between us. We take turns in parenting our mother and there is some dawning that we might have to become each other's mother. What we already are. There are things she does better than me—the forms are filled in and there are timelines established.

When can we expect her to die? We want to know so we can be there.

I am the best at washing our mother. She becomes my baby. In between and when our mother sleeps, we bring each other tea from the machine. Our faces tense with caring. This is almost too much to bear, to exist here, in these weeks, where dying feels so alive and angry. We are pale in shock.

My face is always in states of healing. Today the lids are purple-black—as if I have glossed over them with a make-up brush. They are greasy and I squint. My nose, fat and hooked. I think my nose has been broken, I am sure of it. I am convinced its shape has changed forever. My daughter's father promises me it hasn't been.

'But look at the way it bends.'

'Trust me, you'd know—that's just swelling.'

I notice I have stopped talking to people—my friends. I haven't been drinking for months and my life is this—looking after Sylvie and fighting—mothering and hurting. I teach in between, turning up to lectures with bruising and scabbing on my knuckles. I never mention it.

And then one morning we all find out the fight is postponed. There is an issue with the venue and seating, and we have to wait an extra month. I immediately worry and panic, because I have booked a weekend trip to Paris—a treat for myself for after the fight. Something decadent. It was my prize if I won or lost. I was going to use it to drink and eat and fatten up after a strict protein and water diet. Now I don't want to go. I can't think of anything worse than sitting in cafés and eating good food. I am living in a brutal kind of purity, and I have started to enjoy it.

I still turn up to the spar that's been arranged at the gym. There are two girls from another gym waiting for me. One is tall and thin, the other short and muscled. My trainer seems twitchy and I feel I need to represent him, this gym, and all the work we have done.

I am going to spar them both. One after the other.

I go into my corner. I have forgotten to braid my ponytail and I hope it doesn't swing in my face. I wear a band across my head to keep the fringe out of my eyes.

The skinny girl moves well, but so do I. I am learning a little about how to find pace in this ring. To slow down—to throw these endless jabs to make space, create range—to make contact. The rounds end, I drink water and take a minute. I am told to count my jabs—to try and throw at least 21 in this next round. It is specific and helpful. He tells me it's likely I have given her a black eye. This feels good. I have not got a mark on my face. The next girl walks in. She is punching her gloves together and looking spiteful—she wears a headguard too and a skintight top and bottom, hotpants that make her look naked. She is hot, sexy. She is bouncing in her corner, foot to foot, looking like she's ready for some war I wasn't told about.

We begin and she keeps trying to land overhand rights to the side of my head. I jab her away, but she keeps coming at me.

My daughter's father was right. I needed to be hurt to know how not to be hurt. It's a language. One of her right hands catches me—but I learn to move my head. Like I've always been told... 'It's fucking standard.' I learn how to use my height against her, and don't join the fight she wants to have. I remember how it feels to be smashed in the face and I avoid it now. I step and skip back into my space so that I can circle her and find ways to jab at her head.

She keeps attacking me, trying to knock me out. She is strong and aggressive. She throws a right and I push the punch back with my gloves. She falls. I am surprised—I pause for a moment. I wonder if I'm supposed to help her up. I look for my trainer. He smiles. She gets up and comes back harder, angry and ashamed, but there is less than a minute to go and I feel bouncy, easy. I am enjoying myself. I let her come to me. She lands a couple of thick, slug shots, but there are seconds left, and I absorb them.

At the end we hug and get a photo and it all feels friendly. It is friendly. There is real respect after sparring, usually. It's the first time I haven't been battered and beaten up and I am relieved. They huddle and make small talk and I am left out. There are tribes. This is tribal. And when the group leaves, I hang back, knowing I'm not invited to their coffee—but that's okay. I busy myself doing 30 minutes on the bike. My trainer tells me that I schooled them both. His teaching has paid off.

The next day I leave early for Paris, kissing my daughter goodbye as she sleeps. For once there are no new bruises, only old ones. I can blink without it aching. My dad is taking care of her, and I am grateful that he steps in whenever I ask. I am glad my daughter can depend on men to take care of her too. A grandad and a dad who make her breakfast and brush her hair.

It isn't until I arrive at Gare du Nord that I put on make-up. I stand in front of the mirror in a tailored black coat. It is from Marni and is newly snug on the shoulders that have beefed up since boxing. My body under these bracing toilet lights is thicker set—there is no soft, chubby flesh. Nothing slinky and feminine. My twenties were spent holding packets of Marlboro Lights trying to be the prettiest in the room. The thinnest—the quietest in her pout—dressed like silhouette and absence. Now I feel strong. I like the slope of new muscle from neck to shoulder. I apply a deep, red lipstick and blue-black mascara over my pale face. I haven't worn make-up in weeks, and eyes and lips pop with this new colour—flesh that seems shinier—there is a new luminosity I haven't seen before. As if everything has grown thicker, lusher. Like wildflower after rain. I am more potent.

I step out into a new city and the Paris light is gold and sweet and slips through buildings with all the memories of my mother and me. We used to come here all the time. Whenever we could. It was our place to be mother and daughter. Us at our best. I walk to the place we ate breakfast and drink thick, hot chocolate from the same wide bowls.

I have missed this—the indulgence.

It is midday and I walk to the steps of the church I sat in when I was first told she had cancer. When there was no more doubt, or hope. Just fact. I lit a candle for her that day, and today I light one more, from the flame of another. This is a thing Mum said... 'Light brings light.' She has become so saintly in her death—all her aphorisms, her soothing sentences—those wise words—they mean even more beyond the grave. They are more concrete, tangible to me now. They are more than the flicker of this flame. I can hear them forever and let tears come. She was right. She was always right, about everything.

My hard body moves through this soft city, and I feel the way it dreams again. It steps with a kind of Paris-swag—a gentle roll, my hair, long and red, and pinned-up, heaped and piled. No braids, no bands. No sweat.

I find a side street bistro serving salad and bread and order a glass of red wine. It has been so long since I had a drink—long for me—it goes down easy. It stays on my tongue—that dark red taste—that cherry and smoke—the glint in the throat when I swallow. Everything is returning to colour—to the old order. And as I sit in the sun by Canal St Martin, I think of how nice it is not to hurt. How much my face takes to make-up when there are no bruises and cuts to paint around. How easy it is, to slip back into my femininity. And how Paris brings that out in me.

After my second glass I arrange to meet friends. They are fun—we always drink a lot when we're together and enjoy dancing and singing into late nights. We see a play first, the four of us, and then head to the 10th arrondissement where we share a bottle of prosecco—and then another. I have two glasses, and as we head back into the night they ask if I want to keep going—to go to another bar. But now I feel drunk, and I walk the 20 minutes home to try and feel sober again. It starts to rain, lightly, and the pavements shine. The feeling I used to enjoy now brings anxiety.

I worry I have messed up weeks of work. I've stepped too far from routine. I was supposed to just slip into the fun and the good food—but now I feel drunk and grubby, and also sad. I forget the way home and it takes me longer than it should. I have the taste of old onion soup and bread and wine and then for reasons I will only be able to think about tomorrow morning I go into another bar and order another drink. I don't need to talk myself into it—I order it easily—my mouth is swollen and plummy, with the tannin and the licking of my lip. I sip this new drink and feel a calm return to my veins—if only temporary, it will glisten the worry and send me to bed.

There is sense and elegance in not ordering another and I make it back to the apartment, alone and in the dark. I am struck by how alone I am. How in another city this is amplified. How so totally my mum is not here. How filling the space is impossible. I take my make-up off. I wipe it roughly, until my eyes sting and the mascara is a smudged shadow around my lid. I look how I have looked these last months and weeks—a little bruised. A little in shadow.

13

*I bring new clothes every time I visit. I go to Peacocks on the high
street. Cheap, soft sets that won't hurt the shiver of her limbs when
she moves, made of fluff, or fine, light, whispering trousers—barely
breath on her skin. Clothes she can have accidents in. Everything hurts
her. When I take her to the bathroom to wash her, the chair needs
piles of towels before she can sit. She feels only her edges. The plastic
of this chair moves her to tears, and she shouts at me. Pain makes her
angry. I am too slow, too clumsy—she wants herself washed quicker.
When I ask if it's okay to wash her in places that are hers, private, she
grabs the flannel and throws it at herself. She yells at me for even
asking. Then she is cold, and I wrap her in the towels that aren't soft
like the pyjamas I have bought for her. They scratch and they ache, and
she weeps to me, and I cradle her, but that hurts too. I dress her over
the drip, trying to avoid the wires. Trying not to snag the feed on her
nose. She yells at me that she has been reduced. She shakes in fury.
I can't hold her. Her knuckles look bulbed and deformed on her thin
fingers and they snatch at air as she tries to raise her body up, holding
onto nothing.*

Back to bed, I take her. She is given morphine, and she is soothed.

And it is like this now. This is how we are. She reaches for my hand, and I hold it open, a cradle for hers, as she falls asleep. We are on a countdown.

I feel shy stepping back into the gym. I perform in ritual, scraping my hair back so it yanks my forehead into facelift—braiding the ponytail into hard rope. Taking off my jewellery and all the rings, I am stripped and serious, as if Paris hardly happened. I still feel guilty for going and drink three coffees to make sure I'm sharp and ready. My trainer waits for me in the ring and I start the session saying sorry. Sorry for drinking the wine in Paris. I begin to try and wrap my hands and he steps in and takes over, doing them for me, expert and graceful—he knows the pattern of my hands and wrist.

He asks me if I had a good time and I nod, but in a way that suggests it wasn't as fun as boxing. I feel bad for seeking out pleasure. My hands get wrapped up, and I bend my fingers and make fists to make sure they aren't too tight.

There is sparring today, but first we need to warm-up—to work on some skills. I sweat out three rounds of punching and keep reminding myself to move after each punch. My height annoys me and I still feel awkward bending low. I don't know if I imagine it, but I feel like I am being praised less than usual. We go to the floor, to the mirrors. I work on double-jabs, over and over, until they are locked into muscle, and until they are extended, sharp—I am working so hard—I want him to be impressed. I want to be brilliant. I want to show him that those days in Paris meant nothing to my body. I bash out these jabs on the bag, until my muscle remembers each one. It is still a surprise to me, to see my face so serious, so able and animal. To pant and groan. I can imagine an opponent now. When I shadow box, the punches thrown into air are aimed at someone's head.

I take a break and wait for my sparring partner to arrive—for a girl to show up. I sip water and stretch—I am almost excited.

A man walks in—the one who did my corner two weeks ago.

I have boxed men before. A few older boxers have walked me through rounds, letting me take jabs at their head. And my trainer has been a constant sparring partner, putting me in holds and clinches, making me work through deep fatigue and frustration—and rage. He says it's the Irish in me when I thrash back and try to knock him out.

Today I'm being given to another man.

'You need to have a few tough spars. I've told him to put it on you a bit, to see how you reply to body shots.'

I nod and start to put my gloves back on.

One of my favourites from this gym is here too. He talks about boxing with wisdom and experience—and the critical insight of someone who knows the ways boxing is different to fighting. He has done both. We are in my corner, and he reminds me to move my head.

'Just keep it moving, Anna.'

My trainer makes a formal warning—that this boxer is not allowed to hurt me too much.

'Don't hurt her.' And he winks and nods at me, 'she's only a girl.'

He grins and seems lovely—a gentleman. He tells me he won't go too hard on me. That he won't hit me with real power. He has a baby face, a softness, but he is muscled and in good shape and despite his manners, he looks ready to fight me.

We dance a little to begin with and I am nervous. The stress falls a little once the first punch is thrown—the first shot of pain. He lands a jab, and my face is hot, and it hurts, but mostly it is shock. I gather myself and move around the ring, catching up with some clean jabs and some flush punches too. I hear that I need to keep sticking the jab—keep my range.

At the end of this first round my nose is bleeding. My face is wet with the sweat and blood.

My corner man dabs me down and says I'm doing well. He is lying, I know, but it isn't the time to tell me off. I'm getting beaten up. It startles me after those days away in Paris and I wonder if this spar might be designed to bring me back to reality.

'But your head—you need to keep moving your head,' he begs me. 'Please—you'll see the difference.'

At the start of the second round, I try and do what he says, and to be more cautious, but I forget to protect my body in the process and feel a couple batter me at my waist. These body shots are designed to slow and hurt—to make these rounds feel slow and difficult. I catch breath and manage to land a neat right to his head. And then I throw in flurries and bunches which he blocks and catches, and they go nowhere. I am tired.

He stings me with another to my face and this time I can feel the blood. It is warmer than sweat—and there is the familiar hollow thud across the bridge of the nose and the sharp pinch of air that hurts like I swallowed chlorine. I reply straightaway, angry, and I punch hard. It catches him.

He is supposed to control his temper. I feel the hurt to the side of my body—it is below my ribcage, a little more to the back than the side. The pain is unfamiliar—it is a new agony. I crouch, crumble. I hold onto the ropes and try and find my lungs. I croak breath.

'Are you okay?'

I think everyone is asking me the same question. It is the end of the round. I keep my head down, breathing, leaning into the pain. As I lift up my head there are tears in my eyes, my nose is bleeding, and the blood has moved to my chin and my cheeks. My hair is plastered to my head, hot and flat. I have never looked this bad.

'You look like a girl on a night out in Newcastle.' My corner man jokes, and I smile, reaching for him, just so I can connect with someone who isn't hitting me.

My trainer says we need to stop. 'That'll do.' He looks worried.

But I shake my head. There is a final round.

'I'm going in again.'

He tells me I don't have to do this. He touches the place I was punched. He asks me if it hurts. I lie to him—I say it doesn't.

'It was just a shock. I want to finish.'

'Anna, stop now. That's plenty.'

But I'm already in the centre and I say I'm okay. I ignore my body.

'Are you sure?'

I nod. One more round, I tell him. I tell myself.

I walk around his steps, doing my best to not get hit. I hear my corner applaud me, but it is mostly because I can't lift my arms. The pain is excruciating.

I ignore my body. It doesn't hurt. I won't stop.

There are 30 seconds left on the clock. I take a few hits, but he is gentle now, as if he knows it went too far. I find strength to jab back, and throw a feeble right, but mostly I stay out of range, and slip under, needing to get to the end of this.

When it's over he hugs me, checks I am okay. I hug back, in pain.

'Thank you,' I say, as I take off my gloves and claw and spit out my mouthguard, slipping my arms between the ropes to find peace. And then I sob, as the hurt comes to the surface, and I feel the bruise, an ache and something else—a slip, or a crush of a small bone. I can barely walk, and the pain is so sudden. I still don't want anyone to know, so I pretend it isn't there.

'Anna.' My trainer takes me out of the ring. He can tell.

'You've got balls.'

I am proud of this.

'You want to get some revenge and throw some body shots at him? I'll make him stand there.'

I touch my hair in the mirror. My face is mottled white and red, the colour of my pain. My skin looked like this during labour. It looked like this when I had panic attacks when a boyfriend would ask why my top was so low cut. When he would call me a dog for showing skin.

I think about the effort and strain it would bring to throw body shots. How impossible it is for me right now. That it would twist at the place that hurts and I burst into tears. For a second, my trainer steps away, as if he's about to get caught with a punch, but then he brings me to him.

A hug.

It is the first time he has ever held me close. I have never needed it more than today.

I lean into him and sob that no one will want to marry me now. That I won't be wanted by any man. It makes them all laugh. My drama and my comedy. My nose is swollen, my eyes, red. The braid slipping from its band like weeds. I tell him I'm sorry for weeping and he tells me never to apologise.

'Never say sorry to me. Say it again and I'll make you do burpees.'

We are back to how we used to be, and even though I'm in pain, I laugh through it.

'Now go on and hit him hard as you can.'

My trainer's belief in me is enough. It is always enough and so I laugh again, and head over to where the young boxer stands, protected, and poised, ready to take the blows. The sacrifice—just so that I can leave here with confidence. Like falling off a horse, he won't let me go until I have got over the fear. I swing loose oozy hooks to his right and his left but it's my hand that rattles—he is unmoved—and the nerves shoot from wrist to waist, yanking at the place I was punched, and I am breathless. And still, I ignore it. I keep hitting him, three more times, to each side. I finish and I want to howl. I get hugs from everyone. The man in my corner tells me I did good. I gulp tears on my way back and sit on the train feeling cold and heavy and sore. I can't get my daughter from school like this and hope her dad can finish work early to help me. He can—but I don't tell him how badly I'm hurt.

'Can you feed her, take her somewhere and make sure she eats?'

He can hear I am hurting. But I say it is just the bridge of my nose that's swollen. Making my voice gargle breath and tongue.

I lie in bed. I can only rest on my right side. There is something aching at my ribcage, each breath hammers beneath the bone and this feels more serious than anything I have done to myself in boxing so far. It is a secret bruise, and I remember from Mum, when I watched her coughing, her paper-chest so feeble and wrecked with effort, that her lung hurt the most through her back and she curled herself into fetal position as if that halved the pain.

14

They increase the dose of morphine and Mum's sleep grew softer—she slept all the time. She lies so still she could be dead, her legs barely a shape beneath the blanket. But the hold-and-release of the feeding machine murmurs in the background, reminding us she is being kept alive. She is always sleeping off this tumour. I lie at the far edge of the bed, like a dog, so my body doesn't weigh heavy on hers. I rest my hand on bone, and we nap together. It's sweet and silent and I always wake rested—but glancing first at her chest, and little heartbeat, to make sure she didn't already die.

I am lucky that the nearest hospital walk-in is close enough to get to on foot. After taking painkillers and waiting for them to work I limp to the reception and lie.

'I had an accident.'

I am embarrassed to say I have been punched. The pain is now making me dizzy, hazy—I sit in the waiting area and share seats with men leaning on crutches. One has a bare foot, swollen and pustulating—the cracked heel perched on a backpack. I am still wearing the clothes I sparred in. I haven't even wiped my face and it doesn't matter. I don't care what I look like. I want this hurt to go.

It takes 40 minutes. I know because I am looking at the clock—counting it down.

Just hold on, I tell my body. I am working out when to take another Nurofen. I am called in after 40 minutes and have to take my jacket and coat off. She takes preliminaries. My name, age—am I pregnant. The nurse's hands are cold. She is careful and disapproving.

'There is no bruising on the skin.' As she presses and holds the sore area. 'Any blood in urine?' I shake my head.

'Does that hurt?'

She pushes a little with her fingers, just beneath the ribcage she presses with her fingertips. It feels like there is a small piece of glass just under the skin.

She checks my breath; a stethoscope is solid and ice on my back across my spine. She presses a little more and asks me to lie down. She checks my stomach, like they did when I first fell pregnant. Little, tender fingertips making their map.

She asks me what happened. I laugh, to normalise and to suggest

I was complicit in the injury.

'I box. I am training for a fight, and I had a spar that was a little heavy. He didn't mean to hit so hard. I got hurt—it's how it is. It's part of how it is.'

She raises an eyebrow and says I can get dressed.

'No man has any business hitting you there.'

I hide my face under my jumper as I get dressed.

'What you have is something we call soft tissue damage. You need to rest. No fighting. No training. I don't know if it's kidney, but something has been bruised under the skin.'

I flap at the sleeves of my coat. I am devastated. My fight is in three weeks. I start protesting.

'No, I can't. I have a fight. This can't happen. I need to get better now. I can't not fight.'

I start to cry.

She hands me a box of tissues and puts her hand on my left shoulder. A small touch—not too invasive. Nothing like a mother. And she says... 'How long do you think you need to get better?'

I can't reply because there is no right answer. Some mascara comes off when I wipe my eyes. When I blow my nose there is blood. Like the crust of old clay, it blocks my nostril. She answers her own question, 'I would not be fighting. If you have to, then I would rest for the next ten days and see if this heals properly.'

She gives me the names of hardcore over-the-counter painkillers and heated pads.

'I won't X-ray unless it doesn't get better. Even if you've broken your rib, you will need to stay still and rest.'

She holds my hands when I leave.

'You must look after yourself. I don't know why you want to fight. Why do you want to get damaged like this?'

I have no answer and I take the paper with the names of the medication I need and thank her.

'I am grateful.' I mean it, but I know I won't listen, or take her advice.

At the prescription counter a chatty woman looks me up and down and tells me she's used the same painkillers.

'They really work.' She studies the way I'm holding onto the counter and finding breath.

'They don't realise their own strength do they.'

She says it so breezily, so casually that I don't, or can't, disagree. I don't want her to feel like I'm not on her side, or that she is alone in being beaten up by men. So, I nod. And then she carries on, safe in the knowledge we are the same.

'I got hurt in the same place. It makes you wince, doesn't it. I call it the baby place.'

She packs up the pills in a bag and hands them over with a smile, but her tone is serious… 'Don't take more than two. They are really strong. Honestly though, they'll knock you right out.'

I make a promise. She holds my hand too, just like the nurse. Sending me back out to the world with some wisdom, some learning. To stop getting hurt.

On the way home I take two of the pills, coated strawberry, and pink, desperate for the relief to begin. By the time I reach home the pills have kicked in and I am exhausted. The fatigue is enormous. I am able to message my daughter's father, and I beg for an extra hour. I sleep instantly. And when I wake it's dark and the buzzer downstairs is constant.

It returns to me—that I might not fight. That I might not be able to and in this strange dream-wake state I begin to cry.

When I answer the door my daughter and her father stand there in pause.

'What's happened to you.'

'I won't be able to fight. I got hurt too hard.'

My daughter hears it all too.

She hugs me and I have to push her away with a horrid kind of gentleness that makes me cry harder.

'It hurts me, sorry.'

Her dad frowns—his deep, dark eyes flash a fury I don't want. It won't help me.

'Where did you get hurt?'

I point to my side.

He is never hysterical—has looked at every one of my bloody faces with a reassuring casualness. This time he is concerned.

'That's your ribcage. No way you can fight.'

I shake my head. I cry. All my work. I can't not fight. I am almost there.

'I have to.'

I explain the spar.

'Who's this guy—I'll give him a tough spar.'
His anger makes it worse.

'No, no he didn't mean it.' I defend. I make it okay.

Because it has to be okay.

I have to get myself back to my bed and lie down. I take another two of the sugary pink pills. My daughter lies beside me. Her hand cautious and caring on my arm—her care instinctive. She was like this with my mum too, sitting at the edge of the bed, careful not to crinkle sheets, or press a thumb too hard on her nana's pulse, as if that would be the thing to kill her off. She would sit still and patient like this for as long as it took my mum to fall asleep. Never uncomfortable—bearing the burden of being the one my mum loved the most at this time.

I think we fall asleep like this. Her hand on my rib. At least, when my alarm goes, I wake to see her beside me, her pyjamas on and the covers pulled across us both. Her dad must have put us both to bed. He has somehow become part of the process—he is expert about the ways the body hurts and heals through violence.

It hurts even to breathe, each time I inhale I have to examine the pain again. I try to take short, sharp breaths. Mum used to do this, rasping quickly until she gave herself an anxiety attack. The ambulance would come and tell her she had to breathe more deeply, but she couldn't, she couldn't bear to breathe at all.

15

She doesn't want visitors. They bother her now. We bother her. I read letters from friends, all wanting to tell her she is loved before she dies. She listens like she isn't going to die, asking me to stack them up so she can reply to them when 'she has the energy.' She can't write. The notes she makes in her floral pad are biro scrawls and scratches. Random words she scribbles down. Her language boiled down to barks and orders. She swears more—at us. It is the pain talking.

The only person she wants to see is Sylvie, her granddaughter, who wears a yellow jumpsuit and a crown of neon pink and yellow feathers she has made herself. Queen of the sun. She has dressed up. There is a sense of occasion. When Mum hears Sylvie's voice her eyes open—it is instinct and impulse and she leans forward, her arms reach out. Any pain is denied. This is her last act of love. And Sylvie, unafraid, brave and moving with the same impulse to love her nana, walking to her: gentle and curious. She puts a hand on Mum's face—caught in window glare. Sylvie climbs onto her lap and into her arms and they sit there, eyes closed, for long enough. Still and together; protective and careful. History and eternity in the funnel of light. My mum, taking it with her. Sylvie, keeping it close. No need for fear. No holding on for a little bit longer. This is their secret. They will last forever.

I can't see the damage because it hides beneath the skin,
I can't map and trace the fade and so there is no progress and
this pain, deep in my body—buried in tissue—simmers, hot.

I take too many of the pink pills and then sleep all day. It is
a groggy, coma sleep, that never leaves me feeling rested. It is a
grief, too. I am having to accept I won't be able to fight. The
death of this boxing body.

I don't tell my trainer the full story yet. Because I don't want to
make it real. In my head there might be a way. My body might
be able to fix itself, just like it has done in the past. Surely, I tell
myself, this bruise will heal. I think of clay and imagine my
muscle this way—able to fold itself over the hurt in bulk and in
layers until it has caked over. Of all the hits to my body this is
the one I am the most ashamed of—because it behaves in secret.
I hate it because I cannot show it off. What is its point—what is
its use, to sit within my body and hold me back. This has just
crippled me. I sleep and curl into my side to avoid pain. And
then when that doesn't work I take more of the pills and hope
the hurt stops.

I take just one pill because it is enough to dull pain but also
lets me move around—I can do all the things I am supposed
to do—take Sylvie to school and collect her—take her to dance
class. Wait for her to finish and sit on the train home, listening
to the ways her toes hurt when she dances—to eat and bath
and get her to bed. I am more clingy than usual. I follow her

around a little more—when she hugs me, I hold onto her, as if her health can make me better.

When she sleeps, I sleep too. She slips beside me, and I mimic her breathing, put my head on her pillow. Hushed purring and deep calm.

I wish I had someone to look after me. I wonder what my mum would say—if she would say this is enough. My dad tells me to stop—but he has always told me to stop.

The next day I tell my friend from the gym—I leave voice notes and he is sympathetic. It makes it worse, somehow. Now it is real. I feel sorry for myself. The same thing happened to him he said. There's nothing you can do but rest.

There will be other fights.

But I wonder if I will get there again.

I have a large heat pad that sticks to the space beneath my ribcage and soothes. When I leave my bed there are two that have slipped off—like old sanitary towels, without the blood. Cold, white lumps in my bed. I collect them up and throw them away, before pressing a new one onto my skin.

I cough and the pain is so bad I burst into tears, and I send the message I never wanted to send. I say I can't fight.

My trainer says if there's anything I need he will bring it. He checks in on me. He tells me it's okay to miss the fight. My health comes first. He keeps asking, 'So where did he hit you then.' And I say I can't sit up.

Even though I am sad—even though I am grieving for my strong, better body, there is relief in telling him. There isn't anything I can do. A boxer is only their body.

This, for now, is over. And there is calm in that. To just simply heal, when that's all the body wants to do.

16

She sleeps. Someone, a nurse, has braided her hair so beautifully. Better than I have ever done. It's like there is another mother looking after my child. It trails her neck, onto her shoulder. Still thick and glossy, despite the wallop of medication in her system. She is Millais. She is Ophelia. She lies beside cards— inside the letters of friends telling her what she meant to them.

She wakes to sip warm squash from a straw. The room is always hot. A woman opposite, Hilda, has dementia and Mum watches her with suspicion—annoyance. As if this is Mum's room only. 'All she does is watch her television,' she says. Still able to make sentences.

And then I improve. Over the next days I start to need less of the painkillers and can get in and out of bed without wincing. I smile more. Being released from pain is magical. My face, for a while, has been fixed and pointed in a mild, every day, agony. An agony that sometimes peaks and becomes sharp. But always dull and tugging. Now there is colour to it again.

I wash. I lie in the bath, the first time in three days, and soak the must and sweat—the decay and the death—of my body in healing. I stroke the skin where I was hit and although it has been tender, it doesn't feel sore. The water helps—plunging my hips below I lower my head and put my hair under to wash it. The water turns grey, my body bone-white. There are other marks I see—the fingers in my right hand scuffed and scabbing and the markings of blue bruises on the top of my left arm where I have been hit—I don't remember when this happened—only that it looks new.

Two days later I feel ready to train again. I have two weeks before the fight.

I am treated tenderly—told to stretch—move slowly. I am watched with caution. I take part in a circuit class, just to top my fitness up. But my trainer doesn't let me do any of the strenuous stuff. He looks concerned. When others squat, or do burpees, he shakes his head at me—forbidding me from that kind of exercise. I stretch out cat-like on the canvas, as everyone else jumps and hits equipment.

He says there is nothing of me. A punch is bound to hurt a ribcage.

I nod. I know how much it hurt. But he seems to want to make sure I know he knows too.

'Are you feeling okay, Lois Lane?'

Back to my nickname. Back to my fight name.

I nod. I think I am okay. I am in one of Dad's T-shirts. It's huge—to my knees. It has holes in its side. I am wearing trackpants stained with bleach from an old decorating day—there are rips at the knees. My hair is in a low plait and I'm not wearing make-up. I have always worn make-up. I have forgotten how to be beautiful. Winning—staying on my feet and moving my head, is better than staying pretty.

And I am okay when I leave. My body doesn't hurt. We talk and decide on a final spar before the fight. It will be against the same woman who beat me up the most—the one who made the cuts and bleeds and bruises. The one who left the most marks on my face. It will be the last kind of combat—the last push—before we wind down and have those days of rest and respite ahead of the fight itself. This will be the last fight of camp—and then camp will be over. And then it will just be the fight.

I go back two days later for the final spar. The gym is full, packed. And when we get ready, they all gather to watch. Just like the first time, except this time they know what happened before. They saw me beaten up.

Perhaps it's because I got so battered before—it was so brutal, so gory—but there is expectation. In a way, this feels like the fight itself and maybe others know this too—there are nerves in the building. I feel them—some kind of ceremony too—some final rite of passage.

This time I take the Vaseline. I spread it over my sockets and down to the crest of a cheekbone. I have learned this is necessary. I have learned too, that I will be hit, and I will be hit hard. I have a good boxer in my corner and my trainer stands close beside him, so he can instruct, without being too close. I will have to get used to fighting without him, but knowing he is there, nearby, is enough.

I move every round. Every second, every minute, I move my head. It feels much more like a dance. I step back taller, I come forward with my back rounded, my feet always at their distance apart. I duck out of corners—I circle her—I slow down. I find my range. I feel elegant, smooth—I feel, for once, I have become my body, and all my height, my long limbs, have finally found a way to work. I am in black. I twist and turn like scorpion armour.

I get hit, but not that much. And when I do, I am not battered like I was before.

There are cheers at the end.

It's done, and I leave. And that's it. Me and the woman hug and she tells me how brilliant I am. She will do my corner on the night. I want to say how much I love her for hurting me—

for that lesson in showing me how to get over her punches. But I don't and instead I hug her back.

Just before I go, and just like the time we met, my trainer steps to me and asks if I want to have two fights, a light, soft fight the night before my real one.

'Think of it as a glamorous spar before the real one. For confidence.'

It's for charity. I feel primed to fight anyone. So proud of my body surviving today. I say yes.

17

We are told the food is confusing her. Her body wants to shut down and pumping nutrition into it is harmful. We are making her body do things it shouldn't be doing. She should be dead by now, probably. The doctor, who tells us he is a Buddhist, sits us down in the waiting area. He says he took Mum for a walk—they had a good chat—she was told what was happening. He speaks like she is the woman she used to be.

'It's confusing for her,' he tells us. 'It's startling her, being kept alive.'

My sister asks if she's ready to go. He nods, 'I think so.'

The question is for us—are we ready to let her go. It takes up to three days once the feeding tube is removed. It takes up to three days for Mum to die. Time has never felt precise and finite. Each morning with her—gone forever. A countdown. Waiting for the third day like doom. We have three days to hold onto her hand, to hear the sound of her breath—to watch her sunken chest rise and rasp and fall. We agree.

I go for a walk around the garden. I keep going past her window, watching her in bed, hooked up to the tubes we are about to take

away. Like it's my favourite painting in a museum. Her still life. She is
mine, but she is not mine anymore. Not at all. She is almost in the past.

These next days are about waiting and making sure I don't hurt
myself. No more training, no more sparring. Just resting and
mental preparation. I busy myself with looking up places to get
my hair braided and my nails done. Now these things seem to
matter again. Now there is nothing else to do with my body. The
canvas is a platform. I will be seen. There is a need to be beautiful
again—more than this—I want to be all things—sexy and violent
and big. I want to be seen. I want people to think they'd like to
fuck me, but also be too afraid to try. It's a superhero moment.

I even look at sunbeds, before deciding the gamble under
bright lights is too great. I don't want to look orange. I stay
pale. I know what I'm wearing. All black. Leggings and a sports
bra and Everlast trainers. I have modelled it all on a photoshoot
Mikaela Mayer had with Everlast, where she wore head-to-toe
black. I feel comfortable—confident. I am fighting twice, so
have modified the outfits. For the charity fight, the top is more
basic—it looks more secure—more structured—but for the big,
real fight, it is strappy on the back. It's almost lingerie.

I get my lashes and brows done. My nails are painted petrol.
For two fights I'll need my hair done twice and I book these
accordingly too. My brain already flitting between two ideas
of myself—the charity fighter and the boxer in black, showing

off to friends and family. The big fight matters—the big fight is my way back to something. I keep it simple for the first fight. Straight braids. For the second fight, I have a consultation. As if it's prom. As if I'm going to the ball.

'Do you want to go all *Games of Thrones*, and have it trailing and bound across your back?' He has just done fashion week and is relishing this—he wants to play with my character—with all the drama. I haven't seen *Game of Thrones*, but I know what the women look like. We agree to the hairstyle. I'm excited too.

I wake for the first fight relaxed, easy. I make sure the bag is packed. Wraps and water and plasters for my little finger that still cracks open and bleeds. The only part of my body that won't heal. I stretch, do yoga and breathing. I take a warm bath, before going to my hair appointment. I am meeting my friend in a couple of hours—she is in my corner. A woman I train with. None of this feels like stress. It feels too easy—it almost feels fun. She and I run the stairs of Charing Cross Hospital every Sunday, getting power to the glutes, keeping me stacked and strong so I don't wobble. It is the same hospital Mum was first treated in—where she first started chemotherapy. Where she also nearly died the first time, when the chemotherapy food supplements raised her blood sugar so high, she collapsed in the bathroom, and I had to sit for 12 hours waiting for her kidneys to work again. My mum had died twice. The first time I was able to save her. I was able to bring her back. She was already hard and stiff, her body knotted up in a coma.

The nurse was too scared to move Mum's arms for the X-ray because by then her body was already frail, broken by cancer. So, I did it. I yanked her from the sockets and turned her body around. She groaned and I did it anyway, telling myself it was tough love. She wasn't going to die if I was there. Even when the doctor took me to the side and said the next hours were crucial. If her sugars didn't drop her organs would fail and she would die—everything counted for the next few hours. I sat there, under savage lighting, listening to the drunk howl at nurses from behind another blue curtain. Mum heard nothing. Her coma kept her safe from the Charing Cross bedlam. For hours I was with her, my hand on her shoulder. Until they told me to take a walk and I did—to a coffee shop in Hammersmith and got a takeaway sandwich. I hadn't cried yet. I hadn't cried at all. As I crossed the road the whole sandwich fell from my hands into the road and I watched it all spill into kerb and pavement and walked over it like roadkill, wondering how I'd managed to drop it. And then noticing how hard my hands were shaking, as I walked back through the hospital doors. My dad had taken Sylvie to the Natural History Museum, and I called in to say it was a waiting game.

'Don't tell Sylvie anything yet.'

She stirred, eventually. And it was like the cancer wasn't there at all. In that moment where she was alive again, coming out of her coma, it was the same as if she'd been born new. It didn't matter she drawled and mumbled and looked at us as strangers. Or that she'd wept because she couldn't find the toilet by herself. She was in our world. She was awake. She had come back to me.

I have lots of hair. Piles of thick, coppery ropey hair. Not straight, not curly—easily matted. I refuse to have it short. It sits just beneath my breasts and gets caught in handbag straps. For the past three months of camp I have worn it in tight, high ponytails, in horsey plaits. I need it controlled for the fight. For the first fight I book myself into a Polish hairdresser near White City. It's cheap and they know how to break up the weight and the length and plait it so tight my scalp shivers. They don't ask any questions—just brush in the spray and fix it so no punch can scuff the hair back into my eyes, or across my face. It helps to get myself into character. I look tidy, neat—more aggressive.

It's only when I pay and leave that they wish me good luck. Like they have been talking about it.

I leave Sylvie with her dad. I head to the Clapham Grand. I don't go to south London anymore and I forget the distance—it's far. It's chaos when I arrive. The venue is huge, and I don't know where to put myself. The woman running the event thanks me, hugs me—I'm doing this for a good cause. Others come up to me. I haven't drunk for many weeks and the stink of beer repulses me. People talk too close to my face and their tongues roll sounds—they say nothing. They shout, and I nod.

A posh spar. That is all this is.

I go backstage and wait. I recognise the gym. My friend is there. Other boxers I know. One of them takes me on the pads to warm me up. We all have a quick medical and I meet the girl I'm fighting. She is built different to me, much wider, much heavier. She smiles at me, introduces herself, and I find myself hostile, cold. I know she wants to be nice to me now, so that in the ring it becomes friendly, and we don't hit so hard. She looks scared of me—sick with nerves. I am cold to her because I need to ignore her. I don't want to see someone so scared. It's not good for me to go easy—and it's not helpful to see her as a person. I get the way professional boxers trash talk—the fighter you fight has to be the other—has to be separate. Has to be an enemy. Always the other.

The waiting is endless. I am almost the last one fighting. By this point I have been standing around, and men and women have come up to me, boxy breath in my face, telling me how good it is that I'm fighting. And then it's my turn. My music comes on— The Roots and Erykah Badu—and I'm having my photo taken. The Clapham Grand is packed, balconies of men and pints—women too. Not everyone is paying attention. There have been so many fights it's stopped being exciting to the crowd. The mob. The groups of boys and their plastic cups. George Groves is a judge on the panel. I watched his fight with Carl Froch when I was pregnant in Montenegro—me and Sylvie's dad tuned in on his phone. I want to tell him—we were there, and you were there too.

I have my friend from Newcastle in the corner. He gives me advice. Jab and then throw a body shot in. Wear her down; wear her out. I do exactly this. At the end of the first round, he says it's working. I smile, out of breath, taking a seat, sipping some water. He makes me laugh. He helps me to enjoy it. But she is heavy. She is hard to push off—so I dance backwards. I jab her and keep her at range, finding spaces to hit her. She keeps leaving her body wide open and there's a lot of her. I keep throwing left hooks to her waist. The headguards we have to wear make me feel sloppy and hot. I want to fight without it—I don't mind the lashes to my face.

I win, I box—I'm the better boxer. Easy. Too easy. At the end, when my arm is lifted, I see George. He lowers to the mic.

'Is it a bird, is it a plane—no it's Lois Lane.'

It feels good to win. But not as good as I thought. Maybe I didn't feel like she was ever going to beat me. My left arm hurts, where I jabbed against her. She was heavy—she pushed back. Somewhere a nerve feels twisted and jammed.

But my trainer is pleased. He stands with the clipboard. The next fight has started.

'I didn't watch,' he says. 'But I heard you were brilliant.' He is running the event and has a clipboard and keeps having to go back to dressing rooms and medical rooms—up and down the stairs. But I wonder if he did watch, a little bit even. I hope he did. He looks pleased.

When I leave, a group of young men, plastic beer cups, smiling, want a photo with me. They're in their Stone Island and flat caps. They tell me how good I was. I stand and pose. My face still flushed, sweaty—marked-up. I am awake and alert and still in fight-mode—but drained. Am exhausted. My legs, treading sludge of old adrenalin.

'Is that what it's like to have groupies.' I laugh to my friend who does the Charing Cross steps with me. 'They just want to touch you. To feel a part of what they saw.'

I am quiet on the way home and feel a deep and lonely insomnia in bed. My body doesn't want to slow down. It's still in the fight. I try to breathe slow, make it steady, but am up staring into an opal dawn, suddenly worrying about tomorrow. I take a sleeping pill. Anything, just to stop me being awake.

18

They've moved her to another room. There is no pretty view. Only the wall of the building beside this one. The bed is closer to the floor. Her hands are going blue. I hold one. The veins plump with nothing. She is colder. Her mouth gapes. A chest of bone. Breath too heavy to lift. I want the last warmth. I want to take her so she's everywhere I go. Not even the slight press of her thumb. I will miss that the most of all. The way she stroked my hand.

It isn't dark yet. There is no moon. They tell us to eat and come back. 'She's almost there,' they say.

We eat spaghetti and drink red wine. Do you think it's happened yet; we all ask. We don't want to miss it. She's still there at midnight and I have to take Sylvie home. My dad stays, lying on a camp bed beside his wife. I know she'll be gone by the morning. I know it.

Nothing hurts, but I feel exhausted. I go to get my hair done and feel silly having it coiled and spun and twisted into braids—as if I am in a fairy tale. It isn't *Game of Thrones*—it's *Rapunzel*.

At home I watch those videos of Mikaela Mayer fighting Maïva Hamadouche—I want to imitate the aggression. It's still my favourite fight. I always liked the way Mayer got into the inside—unafraid, bold, bullying. The way she used her height and power. The way she could have boxed pretty—but didn't always. And she won. I liked the way she won—with anger.

Sylvie's dad drives by to give me a quick talk. He is on edge; I can see it. He gives me an energy drink and tells me to drink it an hour before I go into the ring.

I tell him I'm nervous.

He taps the wheel. Says he has to run errands. He is nervous too; I can see it.

'What would your mum do—what would she say to you?'

He means she would tell me to go out there and show them what I'm about.

It's the first time I've been asked, ever—what my mum would think of me doing this. If she'd approve of it. I don't know. I can hear her saying what she always used to say to me, whenever I hurt myself.

'Oh Anna. Why.'

But I wonder if she'd also be delighted—to see me so strong after seeing me in so much terrible sadness. She'd watched me worry myself sick once. When, after nights of acute terror and stress in a romance that wrecked my body, when I spat blood up in sinks, she would be happy to see me so able. To see me as someone so defiantly not a victim. Stepping out from the past, moving beyond her death—to deliberate blows and punches I can see myself heal from.

Days before she died, she had a final grip on the world and grabbed the nurse beside her bed. She pointed to me, 'She's strong,' she rasped. 'She's strong.'

It was the final thing. The last word. The thing she gave me, so she was wherever I went.

'Go on, girl.' Her fist clenched. 'Go on our girl.'

I paint over the chipped nails from the night before. I watch Mikaela again. Her big, deep hooks. The spiteful right hand. Sylvie's dad has always told me to be more spiteful.

'Let them know about it.'

He drives off. I'll see him at the fight later. My daughter will be there too. My friends, colleagues—I have tables of support.

The atmosphere backstage is chaotic. Rammed with people

from the gym we slide into spaces and put bags down, having hands wrapped. The ones who aren't fighting drink beer and so the feeling is a mix of anxiety and abandon—drunk jokes and nervous giggling. We fidget and there is mild flirting—we are aware of each other's bodies in ways we haven't been before. There is more flesh. A woman and I joke about not wearing knickers under tight lycra as it just rides up and irritates—I say I wear knickers for ballerinas that are seamless to work with leotards. The dressing room we are in is the same one used by my daughter before her ballet shows.

I go to the corridor to do pads. I see the girl I'm fighting at the other end—by the other dressing room. She throws right hands that I hear echo and bang. She is shorter in real life, and wider. She looks thick-legged and tough—muscled. And older than I expected. I have spent my life wanting to be thinner, but now worry I got too thin. I want to be bigger. I hit the pads too hard. I am nervous. We pace the changing room again. The laughter there annoys me, and I am so happy when I see Sylvie's dad walk in. He is wired, up for a fight, even though this isn't his. But maybe it is. That's how this works. He picks up pads and barks at me to hit them. I do—he is buzzing—this is *his* fight too. The room looks at us, unsure of how to be in our commotion. He puts the pads back down and tells me, 'Let her know you're there. Let her feel that right hand. Knock her out. None of this nice-nice jab stuff.'

I walk out to the slow trip of The Roots. I hear my name. I feel my daughter watching me. I stand in the corner. It's a deep, arching breath—it moves my stomach in swells and tides.

The rest is minutes. I don't know the order. There are punches that hit harder than others. I remember throwing those, but I don't remember feeling the ones thrown back. I try and knock her out. I give her a standing count. She does the same to me. And we slug and bash and rock until one of us can't keep going. My legs buckle and I know Sylvie is watching, so I climb back and stand. I have to stand. I have to look like I'm okay. The referee calls it. I'm done. I can walk, I can stand—but I'm done.

And it's him—Sylvie's dad—who takes me out of the ropes, holds me to him, leads me to the dressing room. I am so buzzed I hear nothing but noise and when people touch me, or come close, he moves them away. He sits me down and guards me like a dog. No one is allowed near me. And all that hurt, and all that pain, and all the fights and ruined love, moves to a place where it can live. He is there, when I need him the most.

Today, he is my friend.

I hear my mum speak. 'You brave girl.'

I am hugged and held. By others. I am a hero. A fighter. But I am not fully in the room. I am not sad, I don't cry—I am stunned. Utterly buzzed out. I gave and took real damage. I sip from a straw and it's lemonade. I need to get up. I rise, I stagger to the toilet, dragging my bag. No one stops me. I mumble as I walk.

'I'm sorry.' I say to no one.

'I'm sorry I didn't win.'

I put lipstick on. Spreading it like a paste over a mouth already plumped from punches. It's easier to add than to take away. I can't wipe off the markings. Bruises are brown and pink. They clot under the skin. I hold onto the sink.

'Fight of the night.' As I make my way to the bar.

'Never seen anything like it.'

My daughter finds me. I kneel and hold her. She leans away from me to study my face. Her fingers press the corner of my left eye. It hurts, but I let her.

'Why did you take so long to come out?'

I tell her as much as I can remember. 'I had to talk to people. Tell them I was okay. They had to tell me I was okay.'

She holds my hand. I squeeze so she knows I am alive—I am still strong. The way Mum held mine when she was ill. It made the illness not matter. We were still the same.

'I knew you wouldn't win, Mum. But that's alright. You were still good.'

She doesn't speak to be mean. She is protecting herself. She would have got her hopes up—and it would have hurt her. Instead, she saw her mum get back up. She saw me come back to life. That was the most important part of it.

19

She dies at 11 in the morning.

My dad calls me minutes after it happens and we rush back to her, taking a taxi, as if time is still precious and we might catch her in that in-between place. Hold her before she leaves in full. There might be a way of catching some last breath that stays stuck on her lips. My sister kisses her there when we arrive. Her lips have already gone ash. Her hair is brushed on the pillow, soft down—baby hair. A single silver streak curves across the pop of her cheekbone. I begin to rub cream into her feet and heels as I always have done. Sylvie is happy because they have hung a wooden dove on the door, and she asks if she can keep it for her room. My sister keeps going back into the room. I leave them alone, and walk back to the waiting area, knowing I won't see my mum ever again.

My mum is dead. My own mother. It's so ordinary. I try to recall the details. The things that will paint a picture when I need to find her again. The slip of her body beneath the loose, grey T-shirt. The stillness of a stomach no longer swollen as it moves to find breath. And her face, young again—that's the thing I notice the most—that she's no longer in pain. Her face whiter. So quickly a ghost.

I had no idea about the sadness. All the black days that came after the fight. I didn't know that depression came with concussion—that there is a science to this.

I didn't know that getting buzzed in the ring would shift the brain this way—would put me into such a low state—to a dark place. My trainer takes me for eggs and coffee some days after and I almost cancel I am so ashamed to see him—I am so sorry for letting him down. I don't know how to talk about it.

He tells me I didn't, and he tells me how good I was. But there's sadness to our meeting up—something has been wasted. We both know how I could have made it so different—this ending.

'If you'd just boxed. Just used your jab.'

It's the regret. I can't take it back. I can't make this right.

'If you'd just boxed.'

And then he says something I find haunting because it hits deep and true—beyond boxing.

'You had no business having a fight with her.'

I play with my eggs, unable to eat. The portion on my plate seems enormous. I have lost my appetite, and I am close to tears always. My brain has been interfered with in a way I didn't expect. As if I am in a constant slump—always tired—always about to cry. My dad keeps telling me to go and see the GP, but I don't want to be told off by a doctor again. I can't justify my boxing. And I have a trust in my body—I feel it can make itself better. It always has before.

I turn it over in my head and go over the things I remember. I can recall the ring walk. The opening to The Roots and Erykah Badu getting me out the dressing room door. Those early, pumping seconds where my body moved in waves as I charged myself up—my belly and body undulating as if giving birth again—the primal push to get into this fight. I looked to find Sylvie and waved at her too—at wherever she was in the dark crowd. As if this was fun—a day at the circus. I heard my name a lot.

I remember that first round with the most clarity—the big right hand I threw in the first 30 seconds and the way her head moved back and her feet stumbled and how she looked finished, gazing at her corner, stunned, waiting for them to tell her what to do next.

I wanted to hurt her. I wanted to floor her. I wanted that violence. When I punched her with my right hand, I wanted to knock her out. It was supposed to cause her pain and damage. That's why I did it quickly, to let her know I wasn't just about long arms and jabs. That if she came for me, I'd swing hard.

I wanted her to be broken and out of the fight. I wanted the standing count to be the way it ended and for her to be led away and I remember how surprised I was that she got back in the fight. How angry she was. I later understood that unless you knock someone out straightaway, they often come back harder and stronger and more aggressive.

I have to arrange what I think must have happened. I don't recall pain. Only my strange gallop and lurch where my legs buckled a bit, and I stood back up. You can feel your own bone beneath skin. The shudder of your jaw. And it sparks a rage so deep, so profound, that the body keeps fighting beyond logic. I knew Sylvie was there watching. I knew it mattered that I kept fighting.

When I was sitting down in the corner and sipping the water held to my mouth, I knew that it was over. All I could do was keep throwing. My legs were going and all I could do was walk back into the ring and fight. Or try to fight. And I did. We slugged it out—and I had moved so beyond any calm and composure that I didn't even bother trying to move my head. I didn't defend. I bulldozed into her range and took each one and gave it back. I lunged and pounded and connected and took punches to my face and head.

The left fist to my right ear finished it. They call it the equilibrium shot—it takes away all balance. My back fell onto the ropes and my knees buckled and I held myself to standing again. Desperate to keep going. Telling the referee I could keep going. I wanted to stay fighting until I was wiped out cold. Only then would I believe it was over.

I had no business having a fight with her.

I am not sure if we shook hands after. And I didn't see her again. I haven't seen her again.

Part of me wants to because we shared so much. I'd like to ask her how she felt, the second I hit her in that first round. But she is now a myth from that night—some strange nemesis I'll keep forever.

In the strange hurt immediately after, which was more shame than pain, I found myself wanting protection and I kept looking around for Sylvie's father. I needed a body that hadn't been hurt—that was big, a home—to act like security when I was outside of the ring. I kept smiling dumbly because I didn't have words. I'd had language punched out of me.

I did a tour of the venue before I left to say goodbye and thank you. Other boxers from the gym looked at me and smiled. They kept telling me how well I did—what a warrior—what a hero. But as they said it, they looked sad for me.

'To not stay down the way you did takes something strong and special—you're a fighter.'

I knew they were looking at my face. At the spidery, splintered trails of blood and markings and the bust lip.

I joined my writer friends in the pub afterwards—they'd all come to see me. And walking through Ladbroke Grove after almost felt like it was a normal Friday night. I tried to drink a glass of white wine. It made me want to throw up.

'You were magnificent.'

I smiled back at the table. But I wanted to say... yes, but you didn't do it. You would never do it. You would never do it. You just watch.

I sleep a lot after the fight. It is animal. I wash, eat, and sleep. The world is mute and grey. The school drop-off is the most gruelling. I am stared at, and I am too tired to cover it up with make-up. It is enough just to keep myself clean. Sylvie doesn't seem to mind—she tells everyone her mum is a boxer.

One day I can't walk straight.

I am heading to the front door, down the stairs, and I turn left instead of walking ahead. I have to hold onto a wall and wait for the dark dots to fade into white and for focus to come back.

It's about a week after the fight. This scares me. I try to find the centre again—gravity—balance. Getting back up the stairs feels exhausting and puzzling—there are shapes I can't get my feet to find—and when I get to my bed, I cover myself in a duvet and can feel things spin. I put my head on the pillow but am scared to close my eyes.

I once came back from a rave and had an epileptic fit in my sleep. It was a bad pill. My friend was there to hold me and wipe the spit from my face. The next day I had brain scans, scared in that dark tunnel. It turned out fine, but this alarms me. I am worried I'll fall asleep and not wake again. I have to collect my daughter. I imagine her waiting there for me and I never show, because I've died in my sleep. I set alarms in case. I stare at the ceiling. Sluggish, sad—I don't feel like myself. The bruise presses and pinches the left eyelid. I close my eyes. Just for a moment— just a small nap—just to rest. I wake at the first alarm.

The next day it happens again. And then tears. The same pattern, the fuzzy walk and the confusion. And the tears. I worry this will be my life. This dizzy, spinning body that can't walk in a line.

20

She lies in thick rosehip and willow, and we carry her in cold Covid rain. Two daughters holding their mother on their shoulders, surprised by the weight of a body we saw so vanished. She was hardly there, so how can she be so heavy now. We don't know how to comfort each other. The three of us. We read poems. We can't cry in front of each other—there aren't enough people there to absorb this unbearable intimacy. It feels awkward to weep when there's only us three. Sylvie is in school. I miss her. I should have let her come.

There is no sleep in the immediate. I feel Mum more than ever, but in a violent sort of way. As if I am somehow caught and tangled in her journey. I take rosehips and put them in a glass vase on the piano to dry. My sister returns to America, and I am left alone with the rest of the bouquets and baskets of flowers. For days I watch television as the blooms begin to rot. The water tinting green—the shedding petals—the stems limp. After a week I throw them in a black bag. Only rosehip is kept. Rosehip the protector of love. Of the turning season—the last of October—the end of her.

She is buried in green. A linen dress she bought in France. As beautiful as I can make her. I don't see her body again. I don't want to—I don't want to know her cold. I trust they put her in the gold sandals. I trust they do it gently—place her feet into the leather like she can still feel pain. I trust they lift her arms carefully, in case they tear the paper of her skin, and that she'll be burned in the green dress I gave them to bury her in.

I take four weeks off training. My dizzy spells have stopped. But I need a proper break. I don't want to join in all the boxing chat yet—to sit and wrap my hands and smell the faded sweat.

All I want is my daughter. Her bloom and joy. I want to be closer to her. To hold her, to take her hand. To feel that simple ease of being her mother.

We go to Brighton for a weekend. We have a Sunday roast in a swanky hotel, and I have my first glass of wine. I feel the blush of the alcohol and I loosen, relax. We storm through the arcade throwing pound coins at whatever rides she wants to try. We shoot guns. We throw basketballs. We waste money on the machines that promise cuddly toys. I let her do whatever she wants. I let her try her first candyfloss. I buy her chips and we sit on a bench wincing at the smell of the vinegar she has drowned hers in. We laugh. It is so healing.

She asks me to go on every ride, and I do. The strange rickety rollercoaster and the ride that splashes into water. We spend every summer in New York at Coney Island—the rides are grand, elaborate—but she is just as pleased to be here. And I realise it's just about us—the two of us—being together. The start and end of these rides is the same, wherever she is. The rest is just holding my hand and laughing.

I used to get taken here as a child. My sister and I would go with our dad for a weekend every year. It was a highlight—our dad to ourselves. He would do what I'm doing now, pay for us to go on anything we wanted. Our favourite was the ghost train with its plastic puppets and clanking saloon doors. It was my favourite because it used to terrify me—not the monsters inside—but the idea behind it. There was something so horrible behind its creation. I always felt the wheels could come off. The way the bloodied corpse would smack out of the doors into view felt so amateur, so badly put together. It felt like a very real nightmare.

Sylvie asks to go on it now. I hesitate. I don't want to do it. I am older now, and the fear sits differently. I know things can go wrong.

'Please Mum,' she pleads.

'It's the only ride we haven't done.'

I step into the spinning cart. She is thrilled. I hold her hand. I spend the whole time with my eyes closed, holding breath—I hear her giggle. I can feel the ghouls—the horrors—the man-made-ness of this ride. We leave and I am shaken. It has always frightened me. Behind the ride is someone cruel—unhinged—terrible. She laughs.

I try to laugh too. But I leave the ride feeling uncomfortable.

As we turn back across the pier, to load up on more sugar, more games, we pass the boxing game, the one where anyone can hit the bag and get a score. A group of teenage boys are circling each other, taking it too seriously. They take their jackets off before they belt the small bag with the outside of their fists, as hard as they can—their eyes locked wildly onto the score as if life depends on it. They roar and cheer and they are wild in each moment. Whenever it's their turn they go quiet, deep in conquest and each time their friends make noise. None of them looks like a boxer. This isn't even a fight. They just want to be better than the boy before. It only matters that they hit so hard the numbers go up—the musical climb of those red numbers breaking records. That they can hit the hardest—the highest. That's what they come here for.

'Mum, you do it.'

And I must, of course. Because she's watching me. I say excuse me to the boys, and they break up some space for me, not much. I can feel their closeness. Instead of asking them to move I stand wide, so they are forced to.

'Watch me, Sylvie.'

I take my shot. It's not the hardest I've ever hit, and I am laughing, desperately trying not to take this too seriously, but the numbers go up, and the boys look on. And Sylvie stands behind me, she doesn't want to have her own go on it. Not yet.

The boys say nothing, but they have left more space for me now. They have stepped to the side. I am right in the middle.

She holds my hand as we head back to the hotel. I have come back strong again.

'I think you punched harder than all of them.'

It doesn't matter if I did or not. In her world, I hit the hardest. I will always hit the hardest. The evening comes and the fun of that pier darkens and fades—now it's only groups of boys. Now it's just that noise—those shrieks—those smalls groups of young men pretending to be boxers. Watching their numbers go up.

21

My sleep is thick. She is absent. I am taking sleeping pills, and night-time is blanket-black until I wake. It gives me a break. I miss her so profoundly my body curls like a baby on the bed—I will keep searching for her unless I'm knocked out. I only want to sleep. And time is split this way. I work through unbearable days and wait for the chemical rest that blocks her. I need that—I need for her to be gone. My body has to learn she isn't here.

I go back and train, but I walk in nervous, like the first day of school. I'm congratulated. It was 'fight of the night'. To stay on my feet the way I did took real guts and heart. To keep coming back.

'We didn't know you could fight like that. We keep talking about it. You were hurting her.'

I say thank you—as if this is as good as wining. That I hurt her.

I am wild with punches—it's like I'm still unable to finish the old fight. The hooks try too hard. I want to make noise, power. I'm still so angry. I didn't get rid of it in the ring. The fight made me angrier.

She should have knocked me out.

I get tired quickly. It's because I'm still healing. My nose is still fatter than it used to be. There's still a shadow on the eye. It takes time to get back to normal.

I am invited to have dinner with Sylvie and her dad at his flat. He sees how weak I am, how much I'm still struggling. He cooks a roast, and we all sit together, plates on laps. It's nice. I am sitting on the sofa when I find out he has a new girlfriend. It is a sharp and nasty shock. I am almost sick. I know it's not because I want to be with him—I haven't been with him for over seven years—it isn't that. It's more primal and awful than that. It is a trauma response to something I can't locate.

I feel sorry for myself. Finally. All those headshots. All those decisions with Mum's doctors. All that time holding her hand in the hospice.

He has found love. And I have not. In that second I hate him for being in my corner. I become furious with him for being there at all. For messing with the process. For bringing so much of himself into my fight. I blame him for making me angrier than I should have been—for getting me so bloodthirsty—turning me so brutal backstage. For making me fight like him.

But it was also him who came to my rescue when I didn't know how to step out of the ring. It was him who kept me safe when I didn't know how to walk.

I have not learned how to let go of the things that hurt me. I sit in this pain for too long. All the grief—all the concussion—all the worst of me.

It is boxing that gives me space to think. I train regularly again. I am back with my trainer—his presence is maternal—thoughtful. I tell him why I'm so sad and so angry and he nods. He doesn't interfere with it, and doesn't have an opinion, he just gives me space to let go. And that's enough. He doesn't need to ask for more than what I tell him, and I'm reminded of those early days, when I am sure he would see the scars on my arm, white, jagged as the glass they came from, and say nothing. It provides me with framework—with a scaffolding and building blocks. I am learning how to behave again. To be a person. He nurtures me into being myself. I go back to hitting properly. Clean, cool. I have composure. This is why I took up boxing. So that I could let go. And still, when he introduces me to boxers in the gym, he tells people... 'She's good you know; she can really fight.' My confidence returns and the more I train the more I calm the wild punches, the chaos in my brain. With time, I start to hit like I used to—quick, controlled.

'You want to have a fight?'

I smile. It's like the old days. There's always another fight.

'It'll be like a comeback.'

I'd have the summer to get ready. Already being ushered into that reassuring timeline that moves me forward. I have a sense of where my body will be—of where I'm going to take it—through all that hurt and healing again—it is a comfort.

We are getting ready to go to New York in the summer—I promise to use the boxing gyms there—to try out other trainers. Sylvie and I will have four weeks together—she dances in Harlem, and I find an apartment in Washington Heights. It's in the Dominican neighbourhood. Concrete heat and sweat and different gyms and different men—and me, walking a new map. I am desperate to leave London. I pack my gloves and mouthguard and write to a boxing gym in Harlem. I'll train there. My trainer approves of new styles—new coaching.

At this exact time my sister announces she is pregnant—with twins.

It's a miracle—it's magic, a gift. It feels celestial—beyond this world. As if Mum made it happen. We want to go to my sister immediately—to bring love and care and to hold her belly. Sylvie is thrilled to have cousins. We tell her she's the bridge, the thread to link them to their grandmother. How important she will be. She will have to tell all the stories—she can speak her nana back into this world. She will tell them all about Jill Poppy. Not about the illness, and the way she died, but of all the fun things she did when she wasn't sick. The ways she took care of Sylvie. The ways she took care of all of us. Our blood, thickened by this. The maternal line made stronger. Something bigger than all of us has happened.

But there is heartbreak to this too. She isn't here to put her hand on my sister's belly. When she was dying, she told my sister how sad she was—that she wouldn't get to know her children. I know for my sister this is a deeper hurt than I can understand. I always had Mum there, always had her to come round to make me tea in those early, aching mornings, when I was working out how to feed and sleep. She would leave cakes on the doorstep—take Sylvie for autumn walks so I could sleep.

She's not here and it's brutal. This other beginning—it is so beautiful and at the same time, it hurts all of us.

22

She sleeps under a tree in Prospect Park, small, peculiar in the grass. It doesn't look comfortable, to sleep so deeply. She sits up when the Italian ice cart jangles beside her and spoons the crushed ice syrup into her mouth like it's a last meal. It soothes her coughing. This is Sylvie's first trip, and my mum takes her to a Georgia O'Keefe exhibition at The Brooklyn Museum. She pushes Sylvie around in her buggy, fast asleep. My mum gazing at portraits and Sylvie is hunched and bundled—her cheeks flushed in mid-afternoon nap. She asks to push Sylvie because she says it steadies her to do so. She is feeling weak and tired and pushing the buggy and taking care of Sylvie is a way to stay upright and in the world. We don't know that it's cancer. We can't ever imagine that. When she sinks into grass in Prospect Park that is the beginning of it—that is her ending.

I still don't know where she's gone. If burning her meant she had no way to come back. I wanted her to become stars. But I worry ash became air—and nothing more.

We have a condo. A tiny apartment in the middle of Washington Heights, all the way up on 174th street. The air con circles old air.

We can't open windows. It's opposite a Dominican bakery and every morning I leave Sylvie for a minute to run and get my café con leche. I love it here. The streets stay awake until four in the morning. Girls on stoops smoke weed and talk under full moons and I look from the window, at conversations I want to join, the way they shrug and laugh—I want their advice too. I love their big hair, the long nails. And the bachata that plays from car speakers blasted through rainbow light of sun and sprinklers. It is hot. It's always so hot.

'Hey Mami,' the three women all say at the bakery. Because I come here so much, and they know I have a daughter—they give me cake to take back to her for breakfast. It's a sponge cake with chunks of pineapple.

'You want sugar,' they ask in Spanish. I say a little, also in Spanish, and they stir in one big spoon.

We have been here a week and every afternoon, after Sylvie finishes ballet, we walk the baked, sweaty blocks back up to the apartment, passing sprinklers and bachata and men shaving beards on the sidewalk and already it's so far away from home and London and death and I feel lighter. I wear dresses again.

One day, after dropping Sylvie off in Harlem, I walk back through the heat to the apartment. I order another café con leche and instead of going home I keep going. I walk up towards the Bronx—another 10 to 15 blocks. It gets more

Spanish-speaking—I am more obvious. Rows of fruit—mango, papaya, berries, line the sidewalk—fashion shops selling bright dresses with crystal belts and heels lined with diamonds. I stick out. They call me Barbie.

I am about to walk back when I pass a botanica—a shop where they do readings. There are several of these shops, but I am drawn to this one. It's small, green, bejewelled—the window glitters with deities and goddesses. I walk in and am hit by the oils and smoke—the sage and perfumes. Behind the counter the woman smiles. Her hair is poison-red—she wears a deep blue dress and has tattoos across her cleavage. Bear paw prints. Her nails are neon. She smiles—her mother sits beside her. There is warmth here.

She tells me to browse. We talk. She tells me about her life. I tell her about mine. She holds my hand.

'Find the thing you're drawn to.'

She tells me in a voice that sounds like it never has to be raised. When she talks—she is listened to. She doesn't break eye contact and as I look around the shop, I feel her eyes guide me all the way to Yemaya—The Goddess of the Sea and all else. When I research and read, I find out she is a version of the Madonna, The Virgin Mary—she is The Mother. I buy the picture of her—dark hair and white dress. She walks from the sea like foam.

I have a photo of my mum at home, heavily pregnant with me, her dark hair in bloom—her belly round, ready. She wears a white dress, her legs wading in the sea—she looks beyond so that only the side of her face is in shot. Her perfect profile—her lovely nose. She stares at the sun—to that glint beyond sea, where it slips to sky—waiting to be my mother. Perhaps she already felt like she was. She stands strong in the tide—the foam at her ankles. Her hands hitching up her hem.

'She will protect you,' says my new friend. Her own mother smiles from the chair. Like she has known this all along. As if I was supposed to come in today.

I tell her about men. How it has been. Especially since Mum's death. The bad decisions. The blackout nights. The way I have hurt myself.

'You keep getting it twisted,' she tells me it's the women around me who protect me. To pay attention to that. To let them look after me.

'They're with you. You got a lot of women looking after you.'

I am invited to their family party at the weekend. It's to celebrate Saint Agnes. I leave Sylvie with my sister and get changed in the only nice thing I packed. A long blue and yellow dress, covered in flowers. The gold stacked espadrilles I have had for two summers. I sweat within seconds of stepping out of the shower. Everything sticks—I don't know how to be in this heat. I twist my hair up and walk slowly, stepping over sprinklers and feeling the cool of the water on the hem of my dress.

The shop is decorated gold. Bowls of fruit sit on the table, with honey-wine and wide vases swelling with yellow flowers. A group of men play the drums and a woman swallows from a bottle of rum and spits it back to us in blessing. I give them the bottle of wine I brought for the party. I am hugged, I am taken care of. I sip the rum, the colour of coral, sweet, warm and the women hold me—they dance with me. They spoon food on a plate for me. Eat—they tell me. Before I drink the rum, they want me to eat. They stroke my hair and hold my hand when I stand alone—to let me know I am not alone. They keep me safe. They are all mothers. Tonight, they are all my mother. I have missed women taking care of me.

The rum stirs heat. I hug back. When I walk home, past the girls on the stoop, they tell me goodnight. They watch me walk into the building—they make sure I get in okay. I unzip my dress and collapse on the bed—the air conditioning blows the sticky air into the room. I feel touched by something—drunk, definitely but I also feel held, comforted. My mum can't hold me again, but the world still can. It's another way to turn— something different to being hit, to bruises. The lipstick, the oil and perfume on my skin—musk in this heat.

I fall asleep giddy, tired.

I needed a spell. I needed magic. The place the spirits live, dance, sing. This is where my mum can be. Now I have candles to light. Now I can go to her. There are so many mothers I can talk to.

And there's mine. I see her in the sea. There is her hand, her wedding ring. She places her palm to my cheek, the way I do with Sylvie, when I help her go back to sleep. To rest more. If she could speak, she would tell me... 'It's okay to be tired. This has been a lot for you.' She would say how sorry she was for dying. For the burden of it.

23

We go on a walk to scatter Mum. To field a new map of her. It is one of her favourite walks. It used to be one of her favourite walks. It is November. Almost a month after her death. We have to hike up a huge hill and we slip on wet mud. We all nearly fall, and I clutch Mum's ashes in the small tube we were given to scatter her. When we get to the top, we pinch the ash between our fingertips like flakes of salt and let go, returning her to where she came from, despite not knowing where that is, or where to find her, this feels like a space she would be—between the slip of air and water.

We sprinkle the ash. It is caught by wind. I don't know where it ends up. To make sure she stays where I can find her, I pull apart the earth on top of the hill with my finger and thumb and pocket a little of Mum underground. I cover her with stones, so that I remember where she is. In this spot, when I come back. There she'll be. The beginning of some map we have started.

We don't yet know where she'll be buried. Most of her still sits on the piano, in wicker and willow—the metal plaque bearing her name—her birth and death date. These facts etched on metal. I know she can't sit

on the piano forever. Not so much of her. We take pinches of ash and
plant them in places—spots she used to love—but it doesn't feel soothing.
Instead, it feels like I am scattering her mindlessly, trying to find her
a place to stay. So that I also have a place to go to. It feels like I am
scattering her endlessly, because there will never be a place I can go to.

I try boxing again. There is a gym in Harlem. I buy a bottle of
water for a dollar. I walk quickly—it takes a few blocks—I don't
want to be late. It's a Mexican-run gym and the music playing
when I arrive is loud. Salsa, bachata. I am nervous, but less so now
I've had my fights. I don't feel so clumsy, shy. I feel I have a right
to be here. My trainer is younger—he grins—tattoos and ponytail
and the style is immediately different. I am on my toes more—
the first minutes are spent moving and getting used to the
whole ring. I am so used to standing still.

The heat is instant, thick. My clothes stick to my body. I am
made to skip, with rope and around the ring, until my top is
plastered to my back. My shorts too—as if I have wet myself.
There is a huge wet patch where I have sweated into the cotton—
like I sat in water.

Everything is corrected, adjusted. I am used to smashing into pads
and bags—here I am asked to slow down. To correct my hook.

Over and over again I shadow box my left hook until my elbow
doesn't collapse. He tapes it. I watch it back.

'You see the way it dips.'

I am so tired. The heat exhausts me.

'Vamos, Anna, vamos.'

We go again and again. I work it until I have it right. I work the double-end bag, badly. I miss it, mostly. The sweat creeps into my vision.

'Can I have water?'

I feel English and I feel slow.

I sit and sip from the bottle my trainer gives me, and he smiles. I am melting.

'I'm not used to this.' I laugh at myself and tell him I got bashed up in my last fight. I can hear myself tell him with a kind of relish—I want it known that I can take a punch.

'Because you didn't move your head.'

He motions with his own. It's not admired. It's not something to praise in this gym. Being knocked out isn't a badge of honour. It doesn't even mean you're tough—it means you don't know how to defend or protect yourself.

I think again how easy it was for me to get hit. How I took it so readily.

'No need to be taking so many punches to the head.'

We talk about Heather Hardy ahead of her fight with Amanda Serrano. Because she is known for being a bloody, tear-up kind of fighter, I want to ask him what the game plan will be. Hardy is at the end of her career and Serrano is the superior boxer. Hardy was one of the first female boxers to find celebrity. She is famously photographed butchered, bloodied, post-fight. Standing and ready to go again with a crushed nose and busted eye. Her face in snarl. So much pain it slipped to anger. She can have a tear-up. As can Serrano. The fight will reunite them both—they fought years ago—and there is money for Hardy. It's hard-earned and it will be hard-won. The big fights make the difference—money makes taking punches to the head worth it.

The whole morning makes me feel relaxed. The music, the heat, the gentleness to the training. The total absence of conflict. Boxing as style—it has been a long time since I was able to box without spar. I didn't realise how much my nervous system was bound to it and as I walk back through the hot blocks of downtown Harlem and make it to meet my friend in our favourite restaurant, I can feel the need to fight begin to fall away. And the want to correct myself, and my flaws, begin to feel more important. To slow down. I meet my friend, another ballet mum, for a margarita. The sweat dries in the air conditioning and we joke about the two of us having fights. She used to be a parole officer. She's had a gun. She says you work a job like hers with total confidence. If you don't, that's where the accidents happen. That's when people get hurt—when there is fear. We drink and laugh about it, but it is a profound, other toughness, far beyond my own. She tells me about the fights she had growing up in Harlem... 'I always looked for the glass on the floor, Anna. Found the weapon.'

The next time we train I work on moving my body—my head. At first, I can't. I'm too self-conscious. It almost feels sensual, exposed. More than when I first learned to shadow box. This is a dance and when my hips move, I am told I've done well. I start to giggle around my trainer. He moves me slightly, easy— he makes me feel confident again. He's taken the fight out of boxing, which makes me focus on the art of it. To lean out of harm—to dance back to safety. There's no one knocking me out like this. I can hear bachata. And my trainer dances too. I angle off and do it again. I like it, feeling my body so in control, so confident. There's no anger, only the turning of hips, the dipping of a waist. The smoothness of motion. Even the sweat feels lighter, even the heat feels softer. Only this dance, which needs a partner. He is sweet, this trainer. I feel safe—there is no violence here. Only this dance.

24

I gave birth to Sylvie in light and tropical warmth. I ached, groaned—delivered this baby. She slipped so free in blood and sweat. Mum there, she held my hand and gasped when she saw her granddaughter, as if she was the sun. She was the first to hold her, even before me. I had bled so much I felt dizzy. Mum held Sylvie because I could not—and she held me too. As if she had given birth to us both.

At her memorial I read from a Grace Paley poem. The line...

I wanted to help her grow old.

When I read it to the church I cried.

My sister's pregnancy is healthy—she grows bigger. They grow bigger. We are in New York with her and able to form a maternal circle around her—me and Sylvie. I know Mum isn't here so I try to bind her in that sacred hold.

But there is tension—I am not my mum. My sister makes that

clear to me. We argue. I am not to take on that role. I am only the older sister and there is a big difference. It causes upset when I become too close—when I give too much information based on my own experience.

It is hard for her—I had Mum. I had Mum to do the things that she will never have—the tea—the tucking me into blankets when she knew I needed to nap. Those doorstep cakes. The morning messages to make sure I was coping.

I want to do the same for my sister. I go to the grocery down the road, just by the bridge, and buy her fruit and yoghurt. Biscuits and cakes; bread and fish. We entertain names and I tell her to rest—to be still and stop working.

What would Mum do—that comes up a lot. What would Mum do if she could see us all together like this.

That evening, I leave Sylvie with my sister and go to see a boxing night in Times Square. I would not have done this a year ago, would never have gone to the boxing alone. I would not have had the courage.

I walk in, tracksuit and handbag and sit at the bar. I used to go to these nights in heels, face made-up. I'm here to see the boxer Christina Cruz. She is also my age and tall, lanky—I like her style. I drink a beer and find a spot by the bar. It's a good spot. Christina comes on in satin and sequins and it feels good to be on this side of the ring, looking on. To not be fighting. No seconds out. No win or lose. Just watching it all—so easy—with a crowd and a fanbase who sing and shout for the Hell's Kitchen local. I love watching her win comfortably—the snap of her jabs and her quick right hand. A mariachi band plays for the next boxer. The room swells with pride. No one bothers me. I can stand on my own. I can be left here. I don't have to get out of the way. I sip a second beer and watch three more fights.

The next evening, I go for dinner with my trainer. We know each other now—we have spent five weeks training and talking. We drink margaritas and eat tacos. The lights in the restaurant glitter red and green and I circle my ice with the straw. Lick the salt on my lip.

This is different. I am laughing. I am light. I don't mind that the tacos break in my mouth and spill down my chin. It doesn't matter.

I choose him. I choose his kindness. I choose his hand on my stomach. I choose him to zip-up the back of my dress without me asking. I choose the deep sleep.

I leave him the next morning. It has rained in the night. Times Square glistens. The dawn light is crystal, the morning already warm. The billboards boom in neon. I walk past the George M. Cohan statue—"give my regards to Broadway"— the sun comes up.

I go to a kiosk and buy a giant salted pretzel and a peach iced tea with a bunch of single dollar bills. I don't have enough, and the man gives me the tea for free.

I head to the subway. I tread softly. In my own splendour. In my own film. I want to save this hour.

I remember seeing my mum laugh, finally, after her dad died. As if her soul had come back. As if the girl in her had returned and the grief fixed to her chest and lungs had broken and been thrown to the air like loose petals. She was clear of a sadness, finally.

Sylvie sleeps beside my sister on the large double bed. They sleep deeply. I hear their light snores. Sylvie's hand rests on my sister's belly and although Mum isn't here, it suddenly feels like she is. They hold each other and she holds them too. I leave them like this: a mother and child, bathed in gold, Brooklyn light. I boil a silver kettle on the stove to make strong coffee—it's still so early. It's still so new.

25

She slides and stumbles on the soles of her feet—she can't carry her own weight, and she needs me to take her for a bath. All she eats is pink jelly—she scoops out the pot in seconds. She loves the way it feels down her throat. I bring her another—sometimes Sylvie joins her, and they giggle on a sugar high.

She likes me to open the curtains so she can see the hills and the sky—she has tried to paint them before.

'I didn't know if I should paint the pink sky, or try to do it when the sun rises, when it is crisp, gold.' In the end my mum finds a way to do both. The gold cracks the pink. The painting sits on the piano. Sometimes she tells Sylvie... 'That's where I'll be,' and points to the crease where its bleached copper on the canvas and she says... 'I'll wait there and watch you. That's where I'll be.' It is a detail that feels magic, exact. I read Grace Paley's short stories again. The one about the daughter wanting to see her mother in the doorway after she dies. How correct it seems to me, that place. That holy altar—where Mum stands to see if I need more tea, more time—if I want the door kept open. She was always there—arms folded, patient—witnessing.

She asks me to sit on her bed and she holds my hand. I ask her if she thinks I'll ever fall in love. Will anyone think I'm beautiful ever again. She holds my hand—'when you want someone, you'll have someone.' Giving me all the power. All the decision. Making sure it's always up to me.

The summer has softened me, and I know I won't be fighting on the next show. But it takes getting used to—not waking with the bruises and the blood—the violence on my face. After New York I spend August with my dad in the countryside, by the sea. My daughter turns nine and we celebrate her. It's the start of September but there is still the summer burn, except the evening rusts to sunset. The cider-light reminding us that summer is on its turn. We spend days on the beach, lying on warm stones until the sun sinks into sea. We drink outside. Al fresco pizzas and cocktails. Things glow.

And then I meet him. He is from the sea. He has been swimming all day—his hair salted curls. Warm, kind. It surprises me this meeting. I don't notice him until he is beside me. Or I am beside him. We end up sitting together, close, connected. We have never met before, despite being looped into the same town, and I can't find the details of this beginning. I want to but I hardly remember what I was wearing, or what he wore. I only remember that my bracelet shatters when I speak to him and as I pick up the beads and put each one in my handbag, it feels important. It feels a fairy tale because maybe the scattering beads mean something. A broken curse—a spell undone. An end and a beginning.

The things I notice about him are also signs—his neck and the tangle of necklaces. The shells, the pendants. The ring on his little finger that later becomes the ring on my index finger. The bones on his knuckles, worn, big. As if he was grown from earth and heat and stone—worn by the sea into this shape of a man.

It feels seasonal—the end of summer and a new chapter—right on the slice of autumn but it also feels elemental—he is water—I am earth. He has just come from the sea, and he still has it on his body. I can feel the heat on my back, in my hair, I am baked from this sun. The world is peach—like nectar, like negronis—like sliced oranges, like love. It's almost silly how tinted it all is.

We meet again. And then it seems we are always meeting. As if we have always been meeting. I can't place a real narrative on this time—only that we happen—always, and it is the summer. It is always the summer. It always feels like the summer.

But it starts to ask a lot from me. I worry if I can give anything, in fact, the question I ask at the start—at what might have been the start—is what can I give you. He says only me. All I have to give is myself.

I go back to this, often.

The rest of September plays out this way and I wait for the romance to finish. I think it must be a fling. School begins—my work returns. But we still find each other. Life becomes about working out ways to see him. I keep thinking how different he is, how unusual it is for me to decide on a man unlike the ones from before. There is conflict but he has no temper to control. He does not shout.

What is revealed, through this closeness, this new safety, is my own temper. How much I am still grieving. It always catches me out—I thought I'd moved through it—had found my way to the other side. But this anger returns, and it is that same impulse to fight that got me knocked out. Whatever is still buried is finding its way up. That basement stuff that I forgot to take care of. This relationship exposes it all. The shadows I had kept hidden this past summer.

I try to tackle any problem with noise—to be tough—to be the one who gets heard. His strength is his softness—he absorbs it.

One day I thank him for never raising his voice.

'Why would I ever raise my voice to you.'

I don't know what to do without fight and retaliation. To be left alone with my own rage makes it all the more useless, redundant. I have to cut short old patterns and that hurts too.

My mum would tell me stories of Grandad—he played in a snooker championship and right into his eighties he would get into scraps at the club—he was banned for a while. He had his fire. He would argue just because he could. Just because he wouldn't stand down.

It's in my blood to do it.

It takes me months to learn how not to fight. They become the markers of time—each argument I start, or finish. My tempers and my tantrums.

'It took heart to keep fighting the way you did, Anna.'

I went into that fight so angry. I wanted to knock her out. And sometimes I wonder if I wanted to be knocked out.

I start to learn how to mother myself.

I think of her all the time—what would my mum think of him. Would she be happy I chose him—would she like my decision. She always begged me to be with someone kind. Asked me what I'd do if I was happy—if I knew what made me happy.

'You and your edges. Why do they always have to have an edge. Find someone kind.'

I can't remember all the things he and I have done. All the days are soft. All the times we said I love you—even the first time—moving to air like birdsong before they could harden. I can't remember if it felt like we were telling truth and if that even mattered. The words echo into sameness. The first, second or third dates blend and merge into a pattern of us being, touching—I don't think we ever even called them dates. And if I had to write it all down I wouldn't know the order—only that we happen. That we are happening. The story is beautifully ordinary—truthful. He is the detail. The pinpoint and the everyday-ness of not fighting—how wild and daring and brave it is to not seek out pain so deliberately. To not hurt myself.

It is visceral, surgical, clinical—the way this relationship pulls me into new focus. I direct myself. A new order, I have to teach myself, to tell myself, to be in love. To feel beyond hurt—to see beyond grief.

I have to teach myself to live with her death. To let my mum meet me where I am. I have been seeking her out in some other world, where the dead sit in some celestial silver mist—in suns and moons—the purple slip between night and day—and wait for us to find them. I had never considered she could in fact find me every day. That it was the other way round. She would die and return to me—that I could be her home. How beautifully ordinary that is too. The simplicity of that—no edges—just the softness of her becoming my every day.

It's what she promised. That day on the balcony, when we got her diagnosis, she told me how pleased she was that she could share her love of Grace Paley books with me. And when I asked her how I'd find her—when death was still just in its abstract—she turned to me with such certainty.

'I'll find you. Don't worry about that.'

We'd just found out she had a tumour in her lung and grabbed the emergency pouch of tobacco to make a roll-up to share. It was there for emergencies—break-ups and boys, heartache— recreational drags after a bottle of wine. I rolled it for us in licorice paper. We took puffs and passed to each other. Still in shock—the smoke didn't seem to matter. Only that we were together, like two teenage girls. Mum said until we started the treatment it didn't matter, she joked that the thing was already there. Until treatment it didn't make a difference.

'I might as well have smoked all those years.'

She smoked so beautifully. When she drew in, her bones seemed to glide, to shift, held it in her throat, breathed out and smiled. She had never really smoked, but it was expert when she did. I laughed. We both did, it seemed the perfect way to deal with her diagnosis then.

She said it again, exactly this, on her hospital bed. The thing about finding someone kind.

This is how I see her again. Whenever I need to imagine her back.

'Just find someone kind, Anna.'

I hear her—I hear her pronounced and clear.

Light makes light. Love makes you bigger. And she was always here.

'I'll find you. Don't worry about that.'

She said that—like it was nothing to be in her heaven and single me out. I believed her.

26

It has become easier to let her back to dreams. There she is, three silver hoops in her left ear, hair full and dark. It's not so hard to imagine her. It's always her hand. Always her hand on my face—sitting at the edge of the bed as I sleep. Never words and never a story—just the sweet sense of her. She appears in doorways again. Protective, smiling. Saintly. Where sleep used to be a place of escape, it's now a place to meet her. She never speaks to me—but she is saying this—take it easy, Anna. Be kind. Take it easy. She knows I can trouble the thing that soothes me—she knows I can make it hard. Take it easy. And when I wake, then she is dead.

Since saying no to the October fight, I haven't been hit for months. I miss it. In the mirror I imagine the shades of blue and purple. Where the punches would bleed into bruises on my face. The sharp smack. That shudder in the jaw. Suddenly all the challenges that came with it—the mornings and nights I couldn't breathe and the salt water I'd syringe into my nostrils just so I could sleep—seem less bad. I can't remember the pain it caused. It just feels like it was necessary.

I feel softer—I have been drinking more, eating Sunday comfort food. I am not like I was. My stomach pouchy, my bum rounder with fat. Padded around my hips. I look at old pictures of my muscles, when I was sharp and skinny and strong. She seems more of a girl, younger and more open.

When I go back to the gym I do as little as possible. I have become lazy. I am not as fit. I wear loose clothes, less proud of my body when it isn't cut with muscle.

More exciting is the news that my favourite boxer, Mikaela Mayer, is fighting in Liverpool.

We go, me and him. Our first trip as a pair. I love Liverpool, it's where I went with Mum to watch football. We had gin and tonics in Irish pubs, I'd buy the tickets down back alleys, on the black market. She'd giggle at the mischief, of us being a little bit risky.

It's cold by the docks—grey but electric. I have loved Mayer since I loved boxing. The toughness, the height, the way she hits and boxes—showcasing boxing as style and violence.

He is meeting the men at the gym. I worry at first. But there is nothing to worry about—he meets their machismo with elegance. He wears my fake fur coat as if he is putting the other men at ease—he is a different model of masculinity. The arena is bedlam—full, packed. Everyone is behind their homegirl, Natasha Jonas, except me. I admire her—but I yell for Mikaela. She walks out to The Beatles and it's a kind of euphoria, as if I am

watching a friend, as if I am watching myself. I am excited.
I drink too many rum and Cokes and start yelling louder—until
a man standing in another section hears and starts swearing at
me. Not a little bitesize 'fuck-off' that I can hardly hear, but a big
venomous growl. As if he might want to really hurt me if I don't
shut my mouth.

'Sit the fuck down.'

I don't. I stay standing up. I didn't have two fights in a year to get
intimidated by a stranger.

'Shut your fucking mouth.' He's a scouser—his swear words trip
the air and he is drunk too, so they land hard.

My drink falls on the floor. The plastic cup spilling sticky rum at
my feet.

'Who you talking to?'

It's not a question—I just want to give back. I know who he's
talking to.

He tells me to shut the fuck up again.

My new love tells me to calm. Another man gets up on my behalf
and tells the man to go back to his seat. Other men rear up too
telling him not to swear at me.

I know this—I have this support. But I shout back anyway.

'Come here. Talk to me like that again. I'm not scared of your noise.'

I beckon him closer.

I want him to. I want him to come closer—or for me to get to him—and I want to chin him. I can imagine it, so perfectly. A technical truth—the way my right hand, loaded up with my rings, could smack the nerve patterns of his jawline so perfectly— the shattering of it beneath my fist—and how I would follow with a left hook to his face, to his cheekbone. I know how to—I would know how to hit him properly.

'Who you fucking talking to?'

I am just as loud. My words land hard right back at him.

I welcome his violence. I want to give it back to him. On the other side of this new-felt love—there's the purity of this aggression. I am not surprised to see myself like this—I knew it didn't go away. I still seek the disruption.

The boyfriend takes my hand, as if to soothe, to calm and I realise how stupid and dangerous this all is.

It gets dissolved, quietened—some bigger, local man takes

him away, back to his seat. I turn my focus to Mikaela. She seems to dominate and outbox but does not win. She exits with calm and that tricky word 'dignity'. She accepts the decision, embraces the opponent, and it's over.

But not for me.

That night I get so drunk—and keep trying to assert myself. I burst into tears at the bar after being so boozed up I can hardly stand. This is a teenage kind of drunk, an attempt to abandon myself, the type of paralytic that ends in vomit. Except I keep going. He watches with kindness but I'm aware of how ugly this must look. I lean against tables of men. I walk into chairs. I stop making sense.

We end up in a kebab shop and I shove the meat and sauce in my mouth with nasty hunger—a sadness. A grief. He puts me to bed. I wake, and he is there beside me. The smell of lamb in my hair and in my nails—and the sheets too—sweat and grease and all that rage seeped into linen. We don't sleep together. The morning is quiet. We are thinking about it. It was too soon for him to see me like this. I don't know everything I said to him, only that he also seems fragile in the grey morning, and I wonder what would have happened if I did get into a fight. Would he have had to get into a fight too. Did I make him have to protect me.

I shower in the hotel. I try to steam the night off my body. I am sober, sadder. Ashamed of the impulse, the need to fight back, to take up such public space, to make such a grotesque display of temper.

It makes me feel empty, undone. Misplaced heat and rage going nowhere. I can't find a way to put myself back together and when we go for a Guinness before the train home I can see the hurt, the strain—probably the fear that something could have happened. The Irish pub is bleak and bitter from the night before—the wooden booths still reeking old ale. It isn't a good ending. It marks something between us—my inability to control a temper. The space between us a little tainted, brutish. And I realise, not all men want to fight. Not everyone wants to have a tear-up—not because they can't—but because they don't need to.

Later, back in London, I get the opportunity to interview Mayer for a boxing magazine. It is a small kind of redemption—to be able to talk the fight through with my hero feels like a way for me to deal with my own behaviour.

I ask her why she wanted to fight in the first place and she tells me because it was a way of being good at stuff. We talk about bruises and how she wore them and how we both felt when people asked us why we wanted to have people hit us in the face— to have noses broken and bloodied and flattened and bent.

'But your face.' This has been the response. 'Don't damage your face.'

'You are too pretty to box. I can't imagine you hurting anyone.' It used to be a joke in the gym that I didn't like to get hit. When I sparred, I danced backwards. Mayer shrugs. Fighting is fact. It is her life.

'I always thought it was bad ass.'

She has modelled before. Is sponsored by Only Fans. Female boxers get very little promotional help or sponsorship and it's no surprise the female body has to be sold to keep fighters in business in and out of the ring—bikinis and bruises sell tickets. The more it becomes a spectacle the more money there is. It's as cruel to those boxers on the way out too—Heather Hardy was recently dropped by Everlast after her loss to Serrano. You're only ever as good as your last win. She has now taken on a bareknuckle fight to fund her daughter's college fees. Talking to Mayer I realise how the sell-by date of a boxer's body is very real. A desperateness to stay relevant—of value. Heather Hardy calls herself The Queen of Violence—it sells tickets. I admire her.

Records of bareknuckle fights in London between women go back as far as the 1700s when they fought in public, with a prize sum for the winner. Their womanhood and bodies made into spectacle—more than that, something carnival. Grotesque and deeply violent. New mothers with a suckling baby on the breast asked to beat other women as they leaked milk. They fought barefoot on upturned crates, in ripped nightdresses, often topless. I imagine the filth of it—the smells, the ragged, cracked feet—the throb of nipples still sore from feeding. And all that white cotton and linen, blotted and etched in blood. I went to a school where fights weren't uncommon. The fights between the girls were often cut-throat and shocking. I saw a girl pull another girl down the stairs by her ponytail. This kind of violence was always called a catfight, full of hiss and spit—the clawing of hair and ripping tops, with boys jeering and laughing. Now they take videos too, except then we didn't have those kinds of phones. The crowd would make a circle and push them to fight for longer. Sometimes there was blood, but I always thought the girls looked scared to hurt each other, unsure of where to place punches, as if it wasn't really their fight at all, and that the real anger belonged to the boys watching. The girls were fighting to jeers. The boys found it funny, to see this slapstick version of their war.

Female boxers are still a spectacle—the fascination to see this body and face so greased and swollen and black-eyed—the blood-spattered shorts. In photos they smile, as if it doesn't hurt.

I recall my countless bruised eyes, endless nosebleeds, a split knuckle, and the swollen thumb on my right hand. My jaw dislodged when the nerves in my mouth jarred. I have sparred with men and women and been hit every single time. I have woken blocked up because of bruised cartilage, my nose fat. I have been to hospital with soft tissue bruising around my kidney. They became the small sacrifices for what feels like a spiritually transformative journey. Sometimes, I even liked the way the bruises looked. I know how they got there. I often delivered Sylvie, my daughter, to school, knowing my face was cast in new shadows. I would make sure my boxing gloves were seen in my bag, so other parents knew I'd been training and not beaten up at home.

I tell her I used to get stares when I picked my daughter up from school. No one could believe I wanted to mark my face up that way—to be hit so much that it left my nose so broken.

'My love for the sport trumped vanity.'

We both make the joke that people thought we'd been hit by a man and felt sorry for us. She'd be at the supermarket with her boyfriend, and strangers would make suggestions. We laugh it off, as if neither one of us could ever be a victim of domestic abuse.

My daughter comes in to see her and say hello—she is shy. She knows how much her mum has studied this boxer—tried to replicate, to follow—even down to the Everlast sports bra. She stands by my side and when the interview is over, she asks me when we will see Mikaela fight. She asks if I will fight.

I could just have one more—there could be one more fight in me. Isn't that always the way—the last hope, the last win—the need to score it. What's another bruise. Another crack to bone. What's more blood.

I say maybe one day. The same way I answer her when she asks for a puppy. It's out there, somewhere.

27

I go back to the day she died. To those last weeks before finally watching her face smooth to its grey pearl when the pain had finally gone. In those last months it was so necessary for my body to be close to hers. To return us to mother and child. I would nap with my head at the corner of her pillow, or sit in the chair reading, my fingers lightly touching hers. She would try to touch me too, a hand always held out for mine.

We must bury her, but for now she is okay where she is. Beside a picture of my grandad—taken with her at the races. They share a slip of paper, and she is wearing a diamond ring that is not the one given to her by my dad.

I return to her in moments of light rather than in her darkest hours. When she was very much in the world, I punctuate this time by recalling seconds where it mattered most—when we were at our most sublime, profound—still. The precious quiet between us. I don't need to sleep to find her there. She is with me in the daytime too—she slips into rooms, churches—she is there in my corner.

The men in the gym used to feel like fathers and brothers to me. The performative family. I used them all differently. I have needed their care and support. They have wrapped my hands, soothed me with advice. They have wiped my nose when it bled and braided my hair. The ring has been such a space of definition, yet these feminine and masculine parts have so often merged. The stillness, the contemplative corners, they could feel so meditative and maternal. There was always water and ointment to heal and soothe. There were words to calm rages and disappointment. At my most hurt I held their hands. Instinctively—without the need to be touched in any other way. They were safe spaces. All of them. Training in camp took away any impulse to have sex. When I was boxing, I couldn't commit my body to anything else—as if it belonged to the ring. As if it belonged to the cycle, the loop, of bruising and breaking.

But sometimes the slip. Once it shifted—only slightly— when our bodies became bodies that lived outside of the ring. It was exciting—erotic—wearing the body in a different way. A reminder that beyond the ring, without that scaffolding, our bodies could do other things. That fighting and fucking could so easily be flipped. It didn't happen. It never could. No lines were crossed. No hurt, no mess. I am grateful I got to heal for longer.

I spend the weekend with him. Drunk-on-it, loopy love. I think it's love. I think it's more than chemical. I lose edges and angles. I am sex and sweat and breath. I feel my flesh become soft—un-muscled—fat with love. Each sinew made rounder.

His body is a home, and each groove and ridge are where my hands keep finding him. How I feel about him is like this—all the healing leads to this point. There are no bruises left. My skin is a new, clean map. My body is a different body.

I don't train or fight the same way. The men in the gym stop being brothers. After Liverpool they make fun of my new relationship—they make jokes. Gentle mocking.

The next fight is already being talked about. They're every three months. Four a year. It's in spring. I'd have two months if I started now. Time for me to get fit—to spar. There is already someone lined up for me and it's seductive—this conversation. It flatters me. If I wanted to do it, I could.

'You'd batter her—long as you just box.'

I don't say anything. I allow for the pause—and the doubt too. That comes with waiting. It comes with not fighting. I have left it too long.

'Gumshield on. In the ring.'

My trainer tells me we're going to spar.

'Who am I sparring?'

'Me.'

The gym has a few watchers gathering for this. I go to my bag, ready to get my shield. It's been months. It's been three months since I had a spar. It's a long time. I didn't prepare for this.

I can't do it. The thing I need to hurt someone isn't there. I used to love sparring him. Eight rounds of it. I loved the panic and the butterflies. The seconds before the bell—when I knew what was coming. It was a playtime. I knew he'd never hurt me really.

'Sorry.' He used to say. If he caught my nose.

'Don't say sorry.' I'd say, through blood. And send a hook to his body.

But today—something's gone. I don't want to get hurt.

My trainer looks worried. And I don't know what to tell him.

I can't fight.

'Come on, have a couple of rounds.'

I stand there, outside of the ring. And I lie.

'I forgot it, I left my gumshield at home.'

I pack up and leave. I cry as I walk to the station. I don't want to do it anymore. I don't want to hit anyone. This is a loss.

I have been hurt and got better again, got used to feeling broken, raw. I won a fight and lost a fight and felt the full theatre of it. I pressed at my own resilience and vulnerability until bleeding and bruising became normal. I got to take charge of how I got hurt and how I healed. I was the pretty girl and then I was the ugly girl. I got beaten up, again and again. All the time. I learned my body could fill space this way. Boxing offered a new discipline and curiosity about limits and the self. The opposite of abstract speech. The other side of dying. Boxing was constantly living. Narrative in a shifting world. Boxing was the story that could override it all, just for a little bit. The constant, absolute repair. It shed dead cells. Boxing was my story. This is an ending.

28

This is how I can remember her now—we are in Paris. She seems so alive. It is before her pain—before illness. She orders us kir with cassis. Jewels in flutes. I see her in the blur and the sepia of old film. She is ink and glow. The ruby gleam in glass—out of her hospice bed—away from the grey, English window. Not coughing tumours but laughing into glittered sunlight. Cheekbone and charcoal—smiles and lines. Here she is beside me. And we talk in real time. She speaks, she says my name... 'Shall we have another, Anna.' And we do, we always have another.

I turn it down. Two months feels too soon. I'm not ready for an opponent. To go and do it all again, but different. But when I see the other ladies at the gym spar each other I feel a small sting of envy and sadness. I miss it and them—I want to do what they do. I see the fight I should be in announced on posters and I think I could be on that card too—I could be fighting.

I am reassured that there will be another one. That there is always another fight. But now it just feels in the abstract— something I used to do. But it will always be there—of interest.

I might always step into the ring again.

I just don't understand—why do you want to fight? Why do you want to do that to your face—again?

I want to try and explain that I needed the anger to be seen on the outside—to actualise the pain—to make it about flesh and blood.

I go through my carousel of photos with pride.

I like pictures in black and white best, where the blood stuck its tar from nose to mouth. The way the bruises are different shades of ache—spread across my skin. I like being haunted by the twinges in my ribs—it's a reminder I did it. I got through all that pain.

There have been times when I have been in bed and sex has made me catch my breath—just when I thought my body was healed for good. Where the soft tissue damage from before feels fresh—as if the bone and the bruise are still banging into each other. I declare it—I show off. It's where I was hit so hard—it might never heal. Ribs never heal. I am happy that it's there. It belongs to me.

And I want to say this, to the ones who ask me—you weren't there. You weren't in it. You didn't feel the thrill of that tension and composition, the way I arranged myself for a fight. You don't know how easy it became, to hit someone hard. What little pain you feel the moment you get hit back. Only rage—delicious brutal emptying rage.

I am suspended in new love. I mother my beautiful daughter. Spring arrives. I don't fight. I hardly train. Birds sing. Lilac and magnolia bloom tarty and sweet. I give my body the grace to bow out of all of it, to leave it for a while. I've turned down two fights. I have stepped from momentum.

When I visit my boyfriend in the town that he lives in some women treat me with suspicion. I feel inspected. Not all of them, just a few, who seem like they want to know what I'm doing in their town, with one of their own. It's tribal. I stay quiet because I don't know how to fight these fights. That they invade a personal space I thought I'd made so solid.

It seems so beneath all the lessons I learned in boxing—the holding of space and the discipline. I feel too old to go back to this playground. I think of those girls in my school—the fights were always over boys. The way they waited outside the toilets for each other and dragged their victim to the concourse so everyone could see their fight on parade. I think about those women on crates—barefoot and milking and bleeding for the circus.

I wonder if I have put myself in another kind of ring on purpose. Sought out opponents—looked for friction. If I am the one starting trouble and wanting attention. I am the one asking for a fight. Restless, stirring—breaking up stasis—perhaps I am the problem.

All the fights I've had—they were not just happening to me. I was part of it.

And I miss it. I miss boxing. The smell of the gym—the sweat on those bags. Tightening my hair and rushing to the ring—late from a school run. Swallowing the hot coffee, burning my throat. Wrapping my hands as I ran. Opening gloves with my teeth. Winking out of a black eye. Laughing with all of them—I miss all that laughing.

'What time do you call this?'

It was my place. It was mine. It was me.

It was where I put it—all my body. I miss being hurt. I miss hurting people.

I still have the things that matter. I have the things I have kept. The deep, scraggy split in my nail—it never grew back after dying in damp gloves for months and months. The bridge of my nose forever tender—always a little blocked. I have kept the blood on my gloves from an early spar—I never wiped it off. It's dry, like rust. I kept my wide, built shoulders—too big for my old dresses. I ripped the silk of one when I tried to take it off because of the muscle. The bruised tissue inside my rib—that's there forever.

And I kept my fists.

I steal moments and shadow box. They are a secret. Three two minute rounds where I work on my jab—body to head—hooks and right hands. Sometimes in my home—sometimes on the street I'll let a little combination go. Two jabs and a right—music in air—loose with it, easy. One two—one two three. It's a shuffle, a dance—it's my rehearsal space. Just in case I ever want to change my mind. Just in case I need to use this body again.

'Keep that jab long, Anna. Use your jab.'

I practice and I practice.

How can you do that to yourself. Why do you want to get your face messed up?

It's the thing I can't defend. The thing I am still trying to work out. I know relationships can end and the ones we love can die. The heart will split inside and in silence. And sometimes we need ceremony. To dance with ritual. To take pain and press it into some heart-shaped bruise.

And maybe I just like a fight.

Epilogue

'Go in that ring and box for three rounds. Show me what you can do.'

I step in, bowing beneath the middle rope. Dipping back up, rising in the ring's middle. It's so hot—the green canvas greasy beneath my feet because of all the sweat before me. Others have just sparred here.

I jump on the spot to warm-up—but then I start slow, little range-finding jabs. Confident with it. And then I open it up—move into different combinations. Three punch combinations. I pivot, move—I look in the mirror at the boxer in front of me—I go for the bridge. I put my guard up. I remember—move my head.

My trainer stares on...

'Nice.'

Never too much, just enough to make me know I am doing something right.

Other boxers come in the gym, but I don't notice who they are—only shapes—I am focused on me. I can hear them muttering to each other. I can hear the beep of each finished round. There was a time I might have stopped what I was doing and stuck to a corner so no one could see me. Now I don't mind who's watching. The red hair braided messily in two plaits down my back—the busted nose—the scrapes across my eye. In a tracksuit I wore the day before. It doesn't matter that I am sore and smell like yesterday.

I am my grandad. His rage and his wild streak—his rangy shoulders and his fists.

'This time box her head off. Stay away from the inside. Watch your temper.'

I let my jab go. Straight, sharp. It cracks the bone beneath the brow.

I don't know who she'll be yet. She could be anyone. For now, she's me. I dance with her, comfortable, easy—it's beautiful to let it go. I catch my own gaze—we stare it out. Shattered eyes, exhausted from training. The moist film on my arms—it glistens under this pearl light.

They move easy, I am more slouched now, my shoulders rounded. The jabs come loose and straight. I pace the ring, finding new ways to tell this story—these three, two-minute rounds. There is a style—a grace—an ease. My mouth makes those noises—the sounds of a body hissing and whipping air.

After six minutes I stop—dazed, deep into my own nervous system—a meditative depth. Punching air until some cosmic pause. I sit in my heat and sweat—taking up space, sipping into quiet. Still somewhere with my shadow.

ACKNOWLEDGEMENTS

This book is for Mum. You told me how strong I was. I see you in those doorways. And for Sylvie, who always went hand-in-hand with her nana so this book is for you too—you are my whole heart. You are the best of me.

To my sister and the twins—you are the beautiful beginning. I am lucky to have my dad to talk to.

Thank you to Nina for seeing all the truth in this book. To Will for his poet's eye—and to Kate for being so divine and wise. Rough Trade Books feels like home. To Sophie and Alice—I'm so lucky to have you in my corner. Love to Loren—my Washington Heights prima and wise woman. To Mikaela Mayer for inspiring me—and to Lavinia for all the right words.

I learned from all my fights—from all the hurt and healing. Thank you to the men who helped me hit harder and made me feel safe. To the ones who encouraged me to fill space with my noise and blood and body.

Especially Calf—you are all that love is. You turned tides. Thank you for showing me it was okay to stop fighting.

ROUGH TRADE BOOKS

roughtradebooks.com

ANNA WHITWHAM

Anna Whitwham was born in 1981 in London. She studied Drama and English at the University of California, Los Angeles, Queens University Belfast and at Royal Holloway, London where she teaches on the MA in Creative Writing and runs a course called 'Writing Men: The Burden of Masculinity.' She was an Observer Best Debut Novelist, and the first female journalist to write for Boxing News. *Soft Tissue Damage* is her second book.